# Run For Your Life

## STRATEGIES FOR THOSE WHO WILL GO THE DISTANCE

By: Angela D. Henderson

All scripture quotations, unless otherwise indicated, are taken from the Holy Bible, New International Version®, NIV®. Copyright ©1973, 1978, 1984, 2011 by Biblica, Inc.™ Used by permission of Zondervan. All rights reserved worldwide. www.zondervan.com

The "NIV" and "New International Version" are trademarks registered in the United States Patent and Trademark Office by Biblica, Inc.™

Scripture quotations marked (AMP) are taken from the Amplified Bible, Copyright © 1954, 1958, 1962, 1964, 1965, 1987 by The Lockman Foundation. Used by permission.

Scripture taken from the New King James Version®. Copyright © 1982 by Thomas Nelson, Inc. Used by permission. All rights reserved.

I have deliberately chosen not to capitalize the word satan or related terms even though it may violate grammatical rules. Other personal emphasis may also violate grammatical rules, and are done so by intention.

Library of Congress Control Number: 2012906280

Cover design by G. David Cooper

© 2012 Angela D. Henderson. All rights reserved.
ISBN 978-0-9854099-0-6
ISBN 978-0-9854099-1-3 (electronic)

Published By:
Mountain-Mile Ventures, Ltd. Co.
Goose Creek, SC

All rights reserved. No part of this book may be reproduced or transmitted in any form or by any means, electronic or mechanical, including photocopying and recording, or by any information storage and retrieval system, without permission in writing from the publisher.

First Edition

*Here's to all of you runners in life's race who thought you could never go in the direction you are now headed. You have come a long way, and, you are closer now than you were when you started! Keep up the good pace, stay fervently focused, and continue to concentrate on reaching the goal. May grace, mercy, and peace envelope all of you who are willing to go the distance.*

*I would like to give a special "thank you" to:
my husband, Keith (I am so glad to be getting out of this with you!);
my sister, Theresa Allen, and friend, Cindy Mellard, for their countless hours of reading and editing;
my brother, David Cooper, who illustrated the cover; and,
my friend, Matt Ciclon, for helping me to put it all together.
We all make a great team!*

# Table of Contents

Introduction: The Mountain and the Mile ..........................5

Part One: "On Your Mark!" (Preparation)

    Chapter One: Setting the Goal ......................................13

    Chapter Two: The Perfect Fit ......................................29

    Chapter Three: Enduring the Pain, Embracing the Dream ....39

    Chapter Four: Time is of the Essence ............................49

Part Two: "Get Set!" (Perspiration)

    Chapter Five: The Mountain of Determination ................63

    Chapter Six: The Decent of Uncertainty ........................81

    Chapter Seven: Affirming Your Position ........................91

    Chapter Eight: Qualifying for the Prize .........................99

Part Three: "Go!" (Participation)

    Chapter Nine: Preparing to Participate ........................115

    Chapter Ten: Give Me This Mountain ........................127

    Chapter Eleven: Kicking Satan's Ass ..........................139

    Chapter Twelve: Recovery and Reflections ....................153

Appendix ........................................................159

# INTRODUCTION

## *The Mountain and the Mile*

"You want me to do what!? Run!?" That was my initial contestable reaction to an uncomfortable assignment that God gave me one unusually cold January morning in my South Carolina townhome during my personal time with Him. I am used to God cleverly having me do some out-of-sorts activities, but for me, this was way out there. You see, there is something you must know about me; I'm not by any means the athletic type. I have always felt that running was just not my thing. Embarrassingly enough, at the time, I did not even own a pair of tennis shoes. Heels were my thing and still are. And I emphatically reminded the Lord of that essential fact. However, I have learned over the years that God's assignments are not mere suggestions. They are exactly what they are -- assignments, orders, His will for my life at that moment, the purpose for my earthly existence. The essential facts about my likes and dislikes at the time bear no weight in the matter. You either successfully fulfill the assignments or pay the unpleasant consequences of watching someone else enjoy the experience of walking in the complete and perfect will of God, while you are unfortunately sitting by the curb only observing the blessings that could have been yours.

There are some other "club members" out there like me. On a regular basis we receive these intriguing assignments, full of mystery and challenge, not to mention a little agony along the way. I want to make it perfectly clear though; we are not the only ones to be labeled "The Elite." However, we are a part of an elite group -- the chosen ones, the ones who heard the call and responded to its immense propulsion in our lives. This "chosen thing," mind you, is not a guaranteed position. Surprisingly enough, this is one that is earned and maintained each time an assignment is selectively given. You see if you choose by your own God-given self-will not to accept the challenge presented, the assignment will be fulfilled, just not by you. God will accomplish His respective purpose on the earth, but we have to make the ultimate conscious decision concerning our participation.

His response to my words was, "You need to learn endurance." Out of my clouded ignorance of what He was so clearly saying I replied, "Endurance? What do you mean I need to learn endurance?" Now, let me share another thing about myself with you. As you continue to read this book, you will find that my goal is to be very real and transparent with you. I am not going to try to impress you with my undefiled

## Introduction

obedience and all-submissive demeanor. I only wish that I could truly confess that I operate in that capacity every time God challenges me. One of my character flaws is that I find myself at times arguing with God (*Like I could really plead my case as to why I should not do that, and He would see my point of view and opt to change His mind!*). I am not boasting about my all too frequent spars with God. It is just my human nature to resist submitting my way for His way. Submitting seldom comes easily for me. Can you relate to what I am saying? If so, I encourage you to read on.

"I climbed Santa Maria! I know how to endure!" I continued to argue my case as if this past amazing feat was going to astound or impress Him. I could almost hear Him chuckle and even envisioned a slight grin on His adoring face as He said, "I'm going to teach you the difference between the mountain and the mile."

Santa Maria is the largest of thirty volcanoes in Guatemala and the third largest in Central America. I had often looked up at her in awe during my many visits there as a missionary. It was as if I could audibly hear my name being called out from her encrusted dome. I knew the day would come when I would have to follow that beckoning voice summoning me and take the challenge to subdue and conquer the over two and a half mile high climb. That day came on February 14, 2007, the day we celebrate love. I set out on an enchanted journey to pursue the

Lover of my soul, who was inviting me to climb the mysterious heights with Him. The adventure was incredible and still has its impression deep in my soul. It took a laborious five and a half hours to climb up and another laborious five and a half hours to slide back down. Yes, slide. The tiny ash rocks kept me mostly off my feet and mainly on my bottom. Talk about a love that will sweep you off your feet! Needless to say, a huge dose of humility was also administered during that memorable assignment as I was with several of my native friends who I have ministered to and taught over the years. Imagine a constant steady motion of your feet flying out from under the rest of your body as you are thrown down on petrified volcanic ash and rock. My audience found it quite amusing. I thought it was really humorous of God to entertain them at my expense. In actuality I was amazed at their skills in mountain climbing, balance, strength and stamina. I learned much from them and through those lessons I was able to successfully achieve that moment-of-a-lifetime challenge.

"The mountain only took you a day to conquer," the Lord reminded me. "The climb, with its peak in sight, was based on determination. But the mile is based on duration. Only those who are willing to go the distance unaware of its timing and uncertain of its path will conquer."

## Introduction

With that being said, I humbled myself and beat my body under subjection to accept whatever God had in mind. Yes, beat. Again, God's assignments are not always appealing. Sometimes you have to just make a conscious effort and firm decision that, no matter what, you are going to be obedient. That is when discipline is formed in our character. If I knew then, what I know now, I would have never tried to reason with God in the first place. As always, during the process of taking the challenge I became aware of just how much I did not know and how much He truly did. His infinite wisdom and all-surpassing knowledge are far too lofty to fathom. For what awaited me was one of the most intriguing journeys of my life. It was during a time of pain, suffering and loss, that I was trained and prepared to advance full speed ahead into my destiny.

I challenge you today to rise up and take hold of the assignment God has given you. Activate your measure of faith and run toward the mark. Do not allow fear or uncertainty to keep you from your destiny. Do not allow stupor or laziness to rob you of accomplishing great feats for the kingdom. Be encouraged in what you will discover between the covers of this book. Look for the strategies that will help you successfully meet the challenge that God has set before you. If you are ready to go the distance, then I implore you to keep reading. So starting now: ON YOUR MARK….. GET SET……. GO! ***RUN FOR YOUR LIFE!***

# Part One:

# "On Your Mark!"

# (Preparation)

# Chapter One

## Setting the Goal

**Brothers, I do not consider myself yet to have taken hold of it. But one thing I do: Forgetting what is behind and straining toward what is ahead, I press on toward the goal to win the prize for which God has called me heavenward in Christ Jesus.**
**(Philippians 3:13 & 14, NIV)**

### The Wave

2009- A year to remember. For some, your thoughts may be more along the lines of a year best not remembered. Whatever your view, I think we both can agree that it was a year of change, a paradigm shift. Inside the minds of our souls we knew that things were not quite going to be the same ever again. Even though change can be uncertain, the results of it can be favorable.

I jumped on the real estate bandwagon in 2005- the golden year for the market. This was a time when business was booming. Anyone and everyone could get a loan. Even the family pet was classified as a business partner on some deals. And, the return on investments was phenomenal. Yes, it seemed like the perfect time to get on board the money train. However, like most great rides, this, too, would soon come to an abrupt halt.

Upon entering the craze, I had asked God for favor. I wanted to be an example of what God could really do for someone whose knowledge was truly limited in their field of "expertise". You see, I did not want real estate to be my life, only to enhance my life. This was another one of those assignments that I was fulfilling out of obedience. I really never saw myself as a salesperson. I could not even sell a top of the line beauty product. Now, that's pretty bad, considering this is a product that practically sells itself. I did try, but I usually ended up giving it away.

When God spoke to me about entering into the real estate profession, I told Him I did not know business. I reiterated that the only thing I really knew was Bible. He then challenged me by saying, "Well, then, act like it! What does My Word say?" Rapidly, Scripture began to fill my mind, and I began to recite what God's Word says that I can do. Suddenly, I realized that I could do this thing through Christ and be confident that He, who was beginning this new work in me, was more than capable of completing it. I wanted to be successful. I wanted to

## Setting the Goal

pave the way for others who may watch my life and realize that if I could do it, they could also.

The favor that I requested was not a difficult one -- not for Him anyway. I wanted to be top producer in my company. Laugh if you must, but that is what I asked and my God responded. The first year, 2006, I was honored as the number three top producer of our West Ashley office. In 2007, I was honored as the number one top producer of our Goose Creek office. Then in 2008, I was honored as the number eight top producer in the state of South Carolina for our company. Go God! Unlike most in this line of business, I never made the first cold call, nor did I solicit anyone for their business. I did not even ask for referrals. God had surrounded me with a great circle of friends and family who allowed me to participate in making their dreams come true while at the same time enabling me to live mine. How cool is that!

Backing up a bit, my husband, Keith, had begun investing in manufactured homes. He and his partner would buy trailers that needed some serious intervention and transform them into rather quaint inhabitable dwellings. "Affordable Housing" is what they called this business. Having many great returns on their investments, they moved into a new level of marketing, land homes. That is a manufactured home with property attached. Again, success!

Do you get the picture so far? The success I had asked God for was manifesting in our lives. The challenges were great but the rewards were greater. We were living a dream and positioned to achieve even more -- or at least on the road to getting there. However, things began to change. The paradigm began to shift. The ship that we thought had "come in" was now beginning to capsize.

In September of 2008, we enjoyed a grand experience of taking our family on a cruise. For our three kids, Zachery, Lance and Meredith, this was a dream come true. Of course we waited for the discounted rates and even purchased tickets on the Riviera deck-that is the deck just before the basement, before water. But, that did not matter to us; we were on a cruise!

During that vacation, I had a dream. In my dream there was a huge wave that was moving towards the boat. It was shaped like the whale's tale smoke stack that was on the top of our ship (I am not sure if there is some symbolism buried in that or if it was just the pizza I ate at the all night- all-you-could-eat pizza bar just before heading to bed). The children and I were in adjoining rooms. We were looking outside of our portholes at the time watching the approaching wave. I told them to brace themselves because we were about to be hit. It was at that moment that the wave enveloped the ship causing it to capsize. As the dream unfolded, we who were once on the bottom of the boat were now on the top; and, we were helping those who were now on the bottom up to levels of safety.

Now, most would consider this dream a nightmare. I have to admit I was a little disturbed by it myself. We still had a couple of days left on the boat; one being a fun day at sea excursion (meaning we were in the middle of the ocean with no land in sight). Those are the days when you are going from one port to the next. Even though I knew it was only a dream, I also knew it had spiritual significance.

I was reminded of the story in the Bible in the book of Mark chapter 4 where Jesus and His disciples were out on the sea. Jesus had asked them to get into the boat, because they were going to the other side. Without question, or if so none were documented, they did just as Jesus had instructed. It was while they were out in the middle of the sea that a great squall or storm arose. I always found this storm to be most interesting. Why? Well, I once had the opportunity to visit Israel with my mother and father; a trip I will never forget. I was very impacted by my tour of the Sea of Galilee. It is in fact just a large lake.

Earlier translations from Greek to English did not have a word for lake; therefore, the word sea was used. However, it is truly just a rather large lake, encircled by land. What is so amazing is that God had allowed a storm to rise upon the lake. The storm was so great that the disciples' boat filled with water. With much effort they tried to bail the water out, but only found their labor to be in vain. It was at the last desperate moment that they cried out to Jesus for help.

Now, realize that Jesus had been in the boat the entire time. So what was up with that? What was He doing? Why didn't He help before now? The story goes on to say that He was sleeping! Do you ever sometimes feel that God is sleeping when you need Him most? Imagine Him right in the boat with you during the midst of your most troublesome storm, and He's sleeping! Well, the disciples could relate. Here they were desperate, hopeless, exhausted and ready to collapse. Why? They chose not to rest with Jesus. What? Rest? During a storm? When your life is falling apart? You have lost your mind! How is that possible?

It is not only possible, but it is what Jesus invites us to do each time we face our storms. He is there. The storm is never meant for our demise. His words to His disciples were, "Let us get into the boat and go to the other side." You see, our mission is to get on the other side of this storm, not caught up in it. However, when we lose sight of the "other side" we tend to look at what is right before us -- a sinking boat quickly filling with water. It was once they were on the other side, that they were able to walk in the authority that their faith had earned for them. They were able to cast out legions of demons and in time saw ten cities come to know the good news about life in Christ Jesus. The storm had a purpose, and they were destined to ride it out.

This became very relevant to me at that moment. I knew that as a family we were going to be hit by this wave that was coming, and we had to brace ourselves. It was not in our own strength that we could face this, but only through the strength that Christ afforded us. Then, after the storm, we would find ourselves on top helping others to reach that same level of safety and security.

## *The Capsized Ship*

Times were great in July of 2008. As a family moving forward to embrace our future, we felt pretty secure. Little did we realize, though, that progress had suddenly come to a complete stop! All the great accomplishments, endeavors, and plans of success were rudely interrupted. The storm had hit, and all that we had built began to break under the crashing waves of a bear market.

Our boat was flooding with the water of distress, debt, failure, loss, bewilderment, embarrassment, and worst of all, doubt. Our first reaction was like that of Jesus' disciples. I often find such similarities between myself and them. No wonder they make great role models for us today. We tried to bail ourselves out as best we could. We used every imaginable resource that was at our disposal; however, we only sank deeper and deeper. We would profess faith in public, but behind the closed doors of our home we were afraid for our lives. We were losing everything. What was going to happen? When would it stop? Worry and concern became our companions. Needless to say, they were of no comfort during the tremulous times. They only intensified the issues that were upon us. Our hearts were heavy with the weight of the change in the barometric pressure of our lives' atmosphere. Where was God? Wasn't He aware that we were sinking?

    I thought my world was about to come to an end. I could hardly breathe, and I felt so weary. It was at that most difficult time that I heard Him say, "Run." Run? Is that all you've got to say? Is that the answer that I've been waiting for? Whatever happened to hearing, "Be still and know that I am God"? Or why did I not hear, "They that wait upon the Lord shall renew their strength"? What about that unexpected check that comes in every other person's mail? Or the rich guy that walks into your office one day and hands you a check for $10,000.00. I've even heard of people having money miraculously appearing in their bank accounts. And, I get, "RUN"? Is that all you have to say to me, God? His reply, "Well allow Me to add run and do not be weary."

## Setting the Goal

I was reminded of Peter; you know, the disciple that was full of zeal as well as full of himself. It was another day, another storm. Imagine that, another storm. Such is the adventurous life we live in Christ. It's not that life in Christ is stormy for they come, the storms that is, regardless of where or in whom you place your trust. It rains on the just and the unjust; that's life on this earth. However, the storms can be adventurous or disastrous depending on what or in whom your hope is anchored.

In Peter's case, during his storm, he chose not to remain in a sinking boat. To prove that He was Who He said He was, while walking on the waters of that storm, Jesus called for Peter to come. For many of us, it would have been a miracle just to get up the nerve to get out of a sinking ship. We would still try to bail ourselves out, thinking it was the lesser of the two evils. Stay in the boat and drown; or listen to God, get out into the water and surely drown. Hmmm? Doesn't that sound ludicrous? But how many of us find ourselves pondering and mulling over that very decision? Hands down, it should be listening to God for Christ's sake! Yet, we still think we can make it work. We have a plan. Give us just a few more minutes. Go figure!

Now, I know that Peter began to sink; however, that was only when he took his eyes off of Jesus. Let's look at the whole picture. He got out of the boat. He did what did not feel natural, and for a moment, walked in the supernatural. His obedience to Jesus' instructions led him to do what was humanly impossible.

For me, running seemed impossible. "Run? What do you mean run?" I remember that response so vividly, as if I had just said it. I am a woman who hyperventilates while carrying laundry up and down the stairs of our three-story townhome. Trust me, running was not even a consideration. Indulging in chocolate? Maybe. Spending what I did not have? That could have been fun for the moment. Running away? Now that was even doable. But just running? Nope, could not see it. After patronizing my sense of humor and allowing me to babble, He finally said, "You need to learn endurance."

Endurance as defined in *Webster's Dictionary* did not make that word sound any more appealing. Check out what Merriam has to say about it: "last…suffer patiently…tolerate." Exciting uh? Just can't wait to get started!

Be real with yourself. Does that sound like anything you would want to do? Well, in all honesty, neither did I. I debated with God for about thirty minutes before accepting the challenge to more or less sink or swim. Now, that I reflect on that defining moment, my most obvious response should have been, "Yes, Lord, I will do it!" My ship was going under; and without realizing it, I was being offered a lifeboat in that challenge.... one I almost missed.

## *Setting the Goal*

Being a novice in this field of athletic training, (or any field of athletic training for that matter), I was clueless about how to get started. I would watch people in my neighborhood as they would take their morning or mid-afternoon or late-night runs. I felt like a stalker just sitting in my car or standing on my front porch watching and studying them as they passed by. It always amazed me how they could just run. It looked so effortless. However, I questioned would I ever be able to do that. Keith would encourage me and say, "Yes, Honey, you will. Right now you are just building up your stamina." Oh joy; there it was again -- that word. Stamina was just another way to say the word endurance.

I contacted a friend in Virginia, Lesley, who was an avid runner. Together we came up with some goals that I could work towards to increase my speed and distance. The plan was to be able to run three miles in thirty minutes. I was to do this over a period of fourteen weeks. Needless to say, she took me very slowly; which was something I greatly appreciated.

It was during the planning sessions that I realized just how important goals are. I have always been an individual who made goals and worked towards accomplishing them, but I guess I never really appreciated them until now. During a time when I had no control over what was happening in my life, this goal was most helpful. I could not change the circumstances I was facing. The storm was happening. The wave was hitting, and I was in the middle of it all. No matter how hard we tried to bail ourselves out, water continued to flood the boat. However, I could run. I would conquer one mile at a time. I could fix my eyes on the goal and not get distracted. I would make the mark.

The apostle Paul was encouraging the church in Philippi with his words in Philippians 3:13-14 (NIV). He wrote,

> *Brothers, I do not consider myself yet to have taken hold of it. But one thing I do: Forgetting what is behind and straining toward what is ahead, I press on toward the goal to win the prize for which God has called me heavenward in Christ Jesus.*

His letter to them was that of exhortation and encouragement during a most difficult time. He was confirming their position in the Lord. Many times when you face lengthy trials, you may question your

## Setting the Goal

place with God. You may begin to wonder if you did something to deserve this. Or does God really care, or even, what is the use in going on? Maybe you find it difficult to look past the event that you are experiencing to see a grander picture.

It is during those times that you must stay focused. You need to maintain the correct attitude found in Philippians 4:13 (NKJV)

*I can do all things through Christ who strengthens me.*

Also, you must be careful where you place your confidence. Many will come to you offering words that sound like good advice. Out of desperation you may even believe that these people are your salvation. Do not be guilty of putting your hope and confidence in fallible flesh just like your own. There is only One on whom you can truly depend; the One who allowed the storm; and the One who can control the storm.

*Finally, my brothers, rejoice in the Lord! It is no trouble for me to write the same things to you again, and it is a safeguard for you...For it is we who are the circumcision, we who worship by the Spirit of God, who glory in Christ Jesus, and who put no confidence in the flesh… (Philippians 3:1&3, NIV)*

*Do not be anxious about anything, but in everything, by prayer and petition, with thanksgiving, present your requests to God. And the peace of God, which transcends all understanding, will guard your hearts and your minds in Christ Jesus. (Philippians 4:6&7, NIV)*

Next, implement the steps of success by not looking back, reaching for the goal, and continuing to keep moving forward.

*Forgetting what is behind, and straining toward what is ahead…. (Philippians 3:13b, NIV)*

*But whatever was to my profit I now consider loss for the sake of Christ. What is more, I consider everything a loss compared to the surpassing greatness of knowing Christ Jesus my Lord, for whose sake I have lost all things. I consider them rubbish that I may gain Christ and be found in him…. (Philippians 3:7-9a, NIV)*

## Setting the Goal

One other thing, follow the right mentor. Find someone who is where you want to be.

> *Join with others in following my example, brothers, and take note of those who live according to the pattern we gave you. (Philippians 3:17, NIV)*

Like Paul, in your quest for endurance, you will be able to say,

> *….for I have learned to be content whatever the circumstances. (Philippians 4:11b, NIV)*

Are you getting the picture? Philippians is just one book in the Bible that is full of hope and encouragement. It is written by someone who knew what it was to endure. His life is a testimony to the all-sufficient grace of a loving and just God. In setting the goal and running during the times of difficulty, you have to know the Word. It is imperative. There is no other substitute. The Word is your runner's guide whether you are a beginner or a seasoned athlete. Without it, your runs will not be successful. You will miss the mark rather than make the mark.

I encourage you right now, today, to make a commitment to yourself to get into the Word. Read it daily, so the Word can get into you. Through it, God will direct your path and set your course. He will instruct you in the ways you should go. He will counsel you and will watch over you. But you must do your part by opening it up and reading what it says. Set your goals, and start running. Your time is now!

## *Distance Strategy:*

**What are you waiting for? What great thing has the Lord called you out to accomplish? Sometimes, we look for Him in the burning bush, or the thunderous voice, or the trembling earthquake. Most of the time, He is not there. It is usually in the still, small voice in your heart that you hear Him call your name. So, what have you heard Him say? What is His challenge? Have you set goals to reach that? Have you made steps toward it? WHAT ARE YOU WAITING FOR? Remember, it's a good time to be you!**

# Chapter Two

## The Perfect Fit

*...and after you have done everything, to stand. Stand firm then...with your feet fitted with the readiness that comes from the gospel of peace.*
**(Ephesians 6:13b, 14a, & 15, NIV)**

### *It's All in the Shoes!*

Okay, now that I had my goals set, I was ready to move on to the next phase of this strategic planning -- equipment. My running coach, Lesley, advised me that now was not the time to focus on cute clothes or fun accessories. Instead, my focus should be on my feet. The most important item I needed for now was a good pair of running shoes. She remembered the ones I wore on my mountain climb and concluded that those would just not do. I kept them in my memorabilia trunk with all my other travel souvenirs and trinkets of treasured memories. She also instructed me to have my feet measured and evaluated in order to get the perfect shoe type and fit. However, being financially strapped, I opted not to take her advice. After all, shoes are shoes, right?

On the morning that I was to begin my initial run, I went upstairs to my loft and opened up the trunk. Aha! There in a white grocery bag tucked under pictures, newspaper articles, plates, journals, and jungle-wear, I found *"the shoes"!* Oh, the memories that began to run through my head. The thought came to me, "These were good enough to help me conquer the mountain, and they will be good enough to help me conquer the mile." Without further thought to what Lesley had cautioned, I put them on and went out the door ready for my run.

During this time of preparation, Keith had decided to join me. He thought that I could use the company, and he could use the exercise. To be honest, I was so glad that we were going to do this together.

We began our workout with a five-minute brisk walk. This was pretty easy and I rather enjoyed it. I remember carrying on a conversation as we walked in the darkness of our neighborhood early that morning. I was excited about this new challenge and wondered where it would take me. Once the five minutes were up, I remember looking at my quartz watch and saying, "Go!" At that charge, Keith and I began our first one-minute run. I held my arm up to my face trying to watch the small second hand tick from line to line. I felt my feet as they pounded the pavement.

## The Perfect Fit

My chest was heaving up and down. Something did not feel quite right. I told Keith, "I don't feel like I'm doing this right."

His response to me was, "You're not." Ignoring that comment, I focused on my watch as the second hand was winding down the first minute. I encouraged myself that the next rep would be much better. I was just warming up.

How could that one minute have been so hard? What was up with that? I mean, I really felt like I was going to pass out or something worse! I could actually hear my feet hitting the pavement. In regards to Keith's comment, I'm sure that was not supposed to happen. Much to my surprise, that two-minute walk went by entirely too fast, and it was time to run again. As I picked up the pace, I began to look at my watch. It was so hard to see the second hand in the moonlight of the wee hours of the morning, as my arm was bouncing up and down with the awkward movement of my feet fervently pounding the pavement. Oh, how I wished that minute would pass!

The fact that I was a novice and knew absolutely nothing about running was painfully obvious. In spite of my limited knowledge, I knew enough to realize that something was wrong. Keith recommended that I look up running on the internet. My response was, "That is ridiculous! Look it up on the internet? I must be really stupid if I have to look up

31

running on the internet! Surely I can run? You just run, don't you? I mean, how hard can this be?"

I did not feel that I was running with the grace or skillful manner of the runners that I had observed in my neighborhood. They made it look so easy. I was intrigued by their ability to simply run. They did not look as though they were hyperventilating or at the point of death. What did they have that I did not?

One more rep and I was done for the day. I dragged myself back to the house; heaving and wheezing with great dramatic flair. I was having a "spell of the vapors" as we southern belles like to say. I went to the refrigerator and gulped down a huge glass of ice water as if I had been in a desert for days. Now, keep in mind, I only ran for a grand total of three minutes, and two minute intervals of walk time. Yes, I was in bad shape.

Later that day, I had taken my daughter and her friend to see a movie. While in the theater, I began to feel sore in areas that I did not realize existed, for example, that tiny little spot in the back of your heel; the areas underneath the ankles; not to mention the inner knee. I thought, "This is ridiculous! I only ran for three minutes and I am falling apart!" It was then I heard the Lord speak to me, "You did not have the proper shoes."

# The Perfect Fit

## *A Lesson in Peace*

With this remark, God had my complete attention. I was totally oblivious to what was playing on the movie screen and sat in a trance like state as I heard God's voice above all else. He began to expound on His comment. He told me that it is of great importance that my feet are ready for such a strenuous exercise. I was told to buy good shoes, and I had not. Therefore, my feet were neglected and not ready for the challenge they were facing. The feet are so important to a runner. Go figure. If you do not take good care of them and see to it that they are properly fitted with the best shoes, then you are setting yourself up for some major injuries; not to mention sabotaging your goals.

I was reminded of Paul's letter to the church in Ephesus when he wrote to them concerning the appropriate attire for a spiritual soldier. He mentioned that the feet needed to be fitted with peace. It was imperative that they walk in peace at all times through any situation. When our feet are fitted with peace, we are ready for the challenges that lay in the pathway of our destinies. Nothing can stop us nor upset our journey. Peace will sustain us and enable us to keep moving forward.

Peace was something I was missing at this time in my life. I was consumed by my situation. Would we lose everything? How was I going to feed my family on $42.00 for the week? What would happen to our stuff? How would this look? Where would we go? And so on, and so on, and so on. The questions and thoughts ran continuously through my head. It was uncontrollable. I went to bed thinking on these things and woke up thinking on them. It was a vicious cycle that I was caught up in and with each thought I was sinking more and more into a sea of despair and utter confusion.

I began to research Scriptures that referenced peace. To my surprise I had known most of them from childhood. As a child, my parents were insistent that we learn the Word of God. They taught us each night during our family devotion time and helped my brother, sister and me memorize the Scriptures. We did not have a great understanding at the time, but we could quote them word for word. The Word of God is so true when it instructs us to teach our children while they are young. The Word does not leave us and it will fulfill its work in us.

I leaned on these precious verses as if they were my only hope in that time of great uncertainty. And, in fact, they were!

*Peace I leave with you; my peace I give you. I do not give to you as the world gives. Do not let your hearts be troubled and do not be afraid. (John 14:27, NIV)*

## The Perfect Fit

*And the peace of God which transcends all understanding will guard your hearts and minds in Christ Jesus. (Philippians 4:7, NIV)*

*You will keep in perfect peace him whose mind is steadfast, because he trusts in you. (Isaiah 26:3, NIV)*

*I have told you these things, so that in me you may have peace. In this world you will have trouble. But take heart! I have overcome the world. (John 16:33, NIV)*

*For God is not a God of disorder but of peace. (1 Corinthians 14:33, NIV)*

When everything seemed to be out of order in my life, I had to remember that God was in control and that His peace was there for me as long as I remembered to put it on. I had to fit my feet and prepare them for the spiritual journey, as well as the physical challenge, that I was experiencing. It was up to me to be prepared.

Shortly after that first run, I was fitted for a pair of running shoes designed to fit my feet perfectly. I discovered that I overpronated my left foot when I ran; which simply means my foot turned inward. Therefore, I needed a shoe that would provide the stability I needed. "How ironic," I thought. In this time when I felt my very foundation being shaken, God showed me I needed stability. I began to take the challenge more seriously and realize that many more lessons awaited my undivided attention. It was a good time to be me, even though my world seemed to be falling apart. I was learning to walk, or run I should say, in peace which was not an easy task. I had to protect my feet both in the spiritual and in the natural. So, as I ran, I would quote Scripture in my head. I could hear my mom and dad speaking it to me and me repeating it back to them. My understanding began to grow as I was driven to run and learn the lessons along the way that God had chosen for me.

No longer was I feeling victimized by my situation, but I was selected by God for this time. This was a preparation for the greater things that were to come. I did not want to miss my opportunity for those things, so I made up my mind to learn the lessons well and move on.

## *Distance Strategy:*

Are you struggling with a lack of peace in your situation? Have the cares of your days caused you to seem a little unstable? Okay, a lot unstable? Then get your shoes on, and get over it! It is time to rise up and get going. Do not just remain as you are. Things will only get better as you move forward. If you choose to ignore the instructions that the Holy Spirit is saying to you today, then you choose to be a victim and in the end you will fail. But, if you choose to listen and receive, then success is a certainty on this unpredictable path where you find yourself today. Be encouraged, and get into the Word. Know what it says about your situation. Believe in what it promises. Remember, it's a good time to be you!

# Chapter Three

## *Enduring the Pain, Embracing the Dream*

**Endure hardship as discipline; God is treating you as sons.
For what son is not disciplined by his father?
(Hebrews 12:7, NIV)**

### *Mile One*

The creditors' phone calls were on a daily basis at this point, and foreclosure on my home was beginning to take place. What once seemed like a great real estate venture was now costing us everything! Our home was tied into another property that did not sell and a domino effect began. It seemed as if there was no stopping one piece from knocking down another. Decisions were being made for us as the sands of time were quickly pouring through the hour glass of uncertainty. When we told our bank that we had made the last payment for a while, we suddenly became what felt like public enemy number one. We could not have felt any more hunted than if our photos were plastered in every post office, grocery store, and shopping mall with the word: WANTED typed across the top.

I had been running for a couple of weeks; and, on this particular morning my goal was to run my first nonstop mile. I felt strong; I felt confident; I was ready for this conquest! Running had become addictive. You see, my personality type is one that easily can become addicted to anything or anyone. Again, God knew what He was doing when He instructed me to run. This was therapeutic and productive at the same time. In my weakness or self-indulgences I could have found other ways to relieve my stress. Codependency would have allowed me an escape through helping others with their current issues while mine remained brewing on the back burner. I could have entered into relationships that would not have been healthy and were more destructive and demeaning than uplifting and inspiring. God knew what it would take to keep me focused.

I never ran alone. Sometimes Keith would run alongside of me. However, God always ran with me. He would speak to me in such captivating ways. He had my full attention. I was eager to hear what He would share and how I could apply those words to my current circumstances. This day would be very eye-opening. I laced up my shoes and started out my front door with my legs kicking for warm up and my arms stretched out to my sides rotating in small circles. Oh yeah, this was the day! That mile was mine. There was no turning back, no stopping. It was a goal that I could control. I could not control anything else that was taking place in my life. I was not in an unhealthy relationship where I could control someone else's decisions or circumstances. Nevertheless, I could control whether or not I conquered this mile. And, the mile was mine!

The route was simple and very familiar: I would come from my driveway and take a right on to Darcy Avenue. In that direction, I would run to the end of the road and then come back up by the house. From the house I would continue to run to the stop sign at the corner of Darcy Avenue and Davenport Street. The stop sign was the goal, one mile. No problem, I could do this. I was ready for it. I woke up thinking about it. I was determined. The latest phone call from the bank was also inspiring. I was mad, really mad. I had the determination to burn the negative energy that it sparked in my war- weary being. I was quickly learning in times like these, the banks are not your friend. They are just as scared and desperate as you. They would try to squeeze blood out of a turnip if they could. Things were out of control, but I could run, and run is what I did.

The winds had picked up that day. It was March. In the low country of South Carolina, the winds come in very strongly from the warming Atlantic Ocean during the third month of the year. They gust at high speeds of what seems like a small category one hurricane. At times the force could knock a person right off her feet unexpectedly, or at the least, gently nudge her off balance. In the face of these winds, simply driving over bridges and overpasses can be challenging, much less running through those gusts.

As I started out my driveway, I immediately discovered that the March winds were not only strong, but sharp. They seemed to cut my face like a knife. I was not comfortable nor was I convinced that I would be willing to endure that sensation for a mile's run. I recall sharing my complaint with God. The force of the wind seemed almost impossible to press through. Its opposition to my quest caused me to reconsider if I was truly up for this run. I heard His voice, God's voice, in the midst of my own thoughts. He encouraged me to keep running and assured me that the winds would soon change. It was necessary for me to press through these winds of opposition and not stop.

About 4/10 into the mile I had reached the end of the street at the cul-de-sac. As I was turning around the bend, an enlightening encounter occurred. The same winds that were once opposing me were now pushing me. Go figure. I felt as though I was being lifted and nudged. At times it seemed I would run faster as they pressed against my back encouraging me to go forward. My feet felt lighter, and my breathing seemed less erratic. God spoke to me and said,

"See, the very winds that once opposed you are now pushing you. I can do the same with your circumstances. The very thing satan wants to oppose you with I will use to motivate you and push you towards your destiny."

Wow, talk about a defining moment! I was finally starting to get the picture of what was taking place in my life and why. God was preparing me for something beyond the moment of pain and taking me to my next destination in His ultimate plan for my life. Did this knowledge make the pain any less? Absolutely not! By this time I was hurting. My feet were tired; my ankles were numb. With this being the longest distance I had run without stopping already, I was more than willing to stop as I breathlessly approached my home.

Home, what a welcomed sight! I could just stop now and feel immensely fulfilled in my accomplishment and greatly encouraged by the word that I had received. It was good and a break would be more than gratifying. That was when I heard God speak. He could read my thoughts so clearly.

"Why would you want to stop now? You have not met your goal? Your goal is to get to the stop sign. You are not there yet. Yes, you ran farther than any other day, but you are not there yet.

What you have done is embraced your pain. I never told you to embrace your pain. I told you to endure it. When you embrace pain, you have to first let go of something else -- your focus, your goal, your dream. When you embrace pain, pain will talk to you. It will tell you, 'Stop! Give up! It's not worth it! Where is your God? You do not need to go any farther. You cannot do it. You have gone far enough.'

Angela, you cannot come into an alliance with your pain! You must endure the pain and push yourself to go the distance. Even I endured my cross. I did not embrace it as if it were all there was for me. Hope was beyond the pain of the cross. I endured My pain, and because of that, there is eternal life for all who believe. You have to get to the sign. That is your goal. Do not let go of the dream! It will have its place in eternal affairs. Do not stop now; you are almost there! You are closer now than you were when you started. Run, Angela, keep running!"

### *Going the Distance*

With those words pouring into my heart and soul, I continued to run. I could not stop. I wanted to, but I could not. My determination was beyond making it to the stop sign. I realized I was running for something of far greater importance. I was running for my life, my destiny, my hope, my peace, my faith, my dreams, and for my God! It was necessary that I continue. This was His plan for me.

I was reminded of Paul's challenge to the church in Philippi, to whom he said,

> *Not that I have already obtained all this, or have already been made perfect, but I press on to take hold of that for which Christ Jesus took hold of me. Brothers, I do not consider myself yet to have taken hold of it. But one thing I do: Forgetting what is behind and straining toward what is ahead, I press on toward the goal to win the prize for which God has called me heavenward in Christ Jesus. (Philippians 3:12-14, NIV)*

I felt as though I could relate to his message of holding on during tough times as he wrote,

> *But we have this treasure in jars of clay to show that this all-surpassing power is from God and not from us. We are hard pressed on every side, but not crushed; perplexed, but not in despair; persecuted, but not abandoned; struck down, but not destroyed. We always carry around in our body the death of Jesus, so that the life of Jesus may also be revealed in our*

*body…. Therefore we do not lose heart. Though outwardly we are wasting away, yet inwardly we are being renewed day by day. For, our light and momentary troubles are achieving for us an eternal glory that far outweighs them all. So we fix our eyes not on what is seen, but on what is unseen. For, what is seen is temporary, but what is unseen is eternal. (2 Corinthians 4:7-10, 16-18, NIV)*

I recognized death was at work in me. This was not a bad thing mind you. This was a death to all those fears and insecurities that held me back and caused me to hesitate in proceeding to next level with God. I had to face some of my worst fears and conquer them. In doing so, the life of Christ would manifest itself more in me.

I began to envision the stop sign in my mind. Though I could not see it with my natural eyes, I could see it in my mind's eye. I kept my focus, not on the pavement or on the many driveways that I would have to pass, but on the sign; which at that moment was invisible and unseen.

I could envision runners as they were nearing their finish line. I saw myself amongst them conquering a great race. Even though this was only my first mile, it would be the first of many more that I would endure. I had determined in my heart that day that I would go the distance. I would run as far as I had to. I was not going to stop. I could not change my circumstances, for this was God's will for me, but I could run. This was also God's will be for me. I was going to run and not stop until I arrived at my destination. I had a mark to reach, a prize to win, a call to answer. Not making it was not an option. I was not a quitter; I never had been. I would rise to this challenge. I would embrace the dream and endure the pain. I would go the distance.

## *Distance Strategy:*

What are you challenged with at this moment? What goal have you been marked to reach? Is pain talking to you? Silence it with the Word of God.

> *"I can do all things through Christ who strengthens me." (Philippians 4:13, NIV)*

There is nothing that you cannot do. There is not a goal that you cannot reach. You can do it! Do not listen to pain. Allow those things that oppose you to motivate you. The winds are about to change just around the next bend. Be determined all the more to reach the mark. There is a great reward waiting for you at the finish line of this run. I encourage you today to go the distance! Remember, it's a good time to be you!

# Chapter Four

## Time Is of the Essence

*As long as it is day, we must do the work of him who sent me.
Night is coming, when no one can work.*
(John 9:4, NIV)

### Time and Distance

As springtime was approaching, I felt this overwhelming sense of needing to accomplish my goal of 3 miles in 30 minutes in 14 weeks at a quicker pace. Time was of the essence, and I did not have the 14 weeks to accomplish this endeavor. I was planning a trip to Guatemala and knew that God was urging me to finish this prior to that trip. With a sense of urgency and zeal to adequately meet the challenge, I set out for the third mile in the seventh week. At this point I had tossed aside the running schedule and was setting physical goals for myself each run. I would count driveways and be determined to reach the next one nonstop, both furthering my distance each run and increasing my speed along the way.

As God would have it, our personal situation was growing worse. We had to trust Him more and more each day. Keith and I began a saying, "I'm so glad to be in this with you." I have to admit, if this had been another time and another place, a trial of this magnitude would have destroyed our relationship. However, instead of taking our daily frustrations out on each other, we began to lean on one another's strengths. We discovered what true partnership was about in business, in marriage, in life. We came to appreciate one another. Each day we would press in to each other with a lengthy warm embrace and declare blessings over our relationship, children, home, business, and possessions. In the past we had always referred to each other as best friends, but now we had an opportunity to experience the true measure of our friendship. I must say, it went a long way. We were tied together as a chord of three strands: Keith, me, and God. It was unbreakable then and still is to this day.

Setting out on my first attempt to conquer a three mile run in thirty minutes, my focus and determination was to beat the clock. I had already mapped out the route and knew exactly where I needed to be and at what time I needed to be there in order to get back home in the 30 minutes that was allotted. Keith was running with me and giving me encouragement that I could do it. With that love, affection and exhortation, together we set out to go the distance.

## Time Is of the Essence

Keith always had the ability to run faster than me. He was very gallant at times and slowed down to my pace to keep me company. Even though his thoughtfulness was appreciated, I never minded him running ahead. I always told him if he felt the need for speed to go on. I would meet him at home. I was not afraid of running by myself, because in actuality I was never truly alone. The Holy Spirit would always keep me company and share many special secrets and revelations with me. I quite enjoyed His presence and looked forward to the times when it was just me and Him.

On this particular run, Keith was way ahead. I could always see him and felt good to know he, too, was there. I had set my mind on the mark and was moving forward at a good pace. As the halfway point came into view, I noticed Keith had already passed it. This threw me for a loop. "What is he doing?" I thought out loud. "We are supposed to be turning around in between the Immaculate Conception church and the Midway Baptist Church." He was running past all of that! I was not prepared to go farther. I was set on what I thought was the halfway point.

With that confusion clouding my mind, I began to lose focus and get extremely perturbed at Keith. Right there on a very busy highway outside of our neighborhood, I began to yell out to him, "What are you doing? You are going too far! I'm not prepared for that!" Before I could finish my words, I found myself stopping dead in my tracks. I just stopped! I once again yelled, "You have ruined my MOJO! Where are you going?"

He turned around and yelled back, "I was just giving you time to catch up, that's all! I was going to turn around once you reached the mark, and then catch back up with you!"

Without me knowing that, I allowed myself to get all side-tracked and distracted in the thoughts that he was leading me farther than I felt I was prepared to go. I had a mark in my mind. That was the turning point, no farther! Yet, I saw him so far ahead. What was going on?

I was very unhappy with my run at this point. Here I was ready to conquer the third mile and the 30 minutes, and I just stopped at the halfway point. That was not a good feeling. I did not meet the mark. How could that have happened? I found myself walking back home. Looking back, I could only imagine how ridiculous I must have looked. Can you just imagine, as you are driving down a busy street you see this grown woman with her head hung low? She is not walking, but stomping like a child, moving her lips as if she were saying words that were not fit to be heard by man or beast! If you can picture this pitiful woman in your mind, then you have a good idea of what I looked like on that less than glorious day.

Later, as I was inquiring of the Lord what it all meant, with a slight attitude adjustment and a more opened mind to my unexpected turn of events, I heard Him share an explanation with me. This explanation was an enlightening moment in my life. You could say that through this disappointment, there was a lesson to be learned. Imagine that!

He told me that I was at a place of no return. From this point on I had received truth and revelation and was responsible for what I did with it. I still had a free will to make my own choices, but I was accountable for my choices and would walk in the rewards or the consequences for what I knew to be right.

He continued to further share that I had my mind set on a goal, but He knew where He wanted to take me. I had to place in Him my ultimate trust and unwavering faith. Even if it looked as though He was leading me to where I did not want to go, I had to trust Him. I had to be willing to go the distance even though I did not know where that would take me. I had to stay focused and not stop until He said it was time to stop. Even when I did not understand and His direction took me beyond what I could fathom in the natural, I had to keep pressing forward.

It was inevitable that He wanted to take me beyond my own abilities, comforts, limits, and mindsets. He was proving to me about His ways.

> *For my thoughts are not your thoughts, neither are your ways my ways. As the heavens are higher than the earth so are my ways higher than your ways and my thoughts than your thoughts. (Isaiah 55: 8 & 9, NIV)*

He told me,

> *If you do not stand firm in your faith you will not stand at all. (Isaiah 7: 9, NIV)*

He was teaching me:

> *Stop trusting in man, who has but a breath in his nostrils. Of what account is he? (Isaiah 2:22, NIV)*

## Time Is of the Essence

You see, up to this point I said I trusted God. I said I would go the distance. I said that I would follow Him through this trial, but now my words were being challenged by His words. Was I truly willing to do what I said? Obviously I was not as willing as I had boasted. When things went beyond what I thought, planned, or understood, I wanted to stop. And, stop is what I did. The run was showing me what was really inside my heart. To be honest with you, I did not like what was revealed to me. I was disgusted with myself and my actions. Could this outward display of childish behavior truly be a reflection of what was inside my very soul? I was not impressed. I was sorry for the way I had reacted so stubbornly and felt genuine repentance in my heart. It was not God who was confused. It was not Keith who was confused. It was me. I was the one who had a wrong idea of how God was to deliver me from my times of trial, while conquering one mile at a time. What a rude awakening! But none the less, I was grateful to have been awakened. Though my methods were wrong, my intent was pure. I wanted to know God more through this trial, and I wanted to get out of it as quickly as possible.

I have always referred to myself as God's poster child for "What Not to Do." For some unknown reason, I usually take the more difficult route of trying things my way first. Then, when all else fails, I check in with God to get His opinion on things. In the long run, I eventually do the right thing and learn a lesson in the process. This lesson enables me to pass along some very helpful insight to others as they are enduring their times of extreme trial. With that in mind, I guess I can say it is with honor that I enter each challenge, ready to learn, move on, and pass it on.

Lesson learned! Now, off to conquer this three mile in 30 minutes goal. Keith was once again in the lead. With the last experience still vividly in the forefront of my thoughts, I made up my mind and set my focus on just not stopping. As we ran up St. James Avenue, I saw the Immaculate Conception Church. With trust, I told myself, "Angela, you are going the distance. If Keith runs beyond so will you. Don't stop! Follow!" I had prepared myself for whatever turn of events I was to face. It was at that moment that I was completely surprised! Keith began to turn around. What? I did not have to go farther? This was the mark? I had made it and now was able to run home?

God spoke to me and said, "That is ultimate trust. That is standing firm in faith. I did not make you go farther, but you did not know that. You were truly prepared to go the distance."

I must say, I was glad to have learned that lesson. I am not the type who usually repeats a class. It may seem like I barely get out of it, but I do not repeat it. Lesson learned!

While heading back home, I kept hearing God speak, "Time is of the essence! You must pick up your speed."

## Time Is of the Essence

I looked at my watch and saw that time was creeping up on me quickly. I still had a way to go. I was getting tired, and my earlier celebration had delayed me a few seconds as I had slowed down my pace. God was reminding me that it was not time to celebrate, but time to work at building up my pace. Time was running out. I had met one goal, but there was still more to reach.

With one minute left, I felt this sensation rise up in me. I began to move my arms at a faster rate. And something amazing happened. My feet and legs moved in sync with their motion. My heart began to race along with the rest of me. I could not believe my pace. I was determined to beat the clock and not have time run out on me or miss the goal that had been set for me.

In great delight and a rush of adrenaline I made it to my driveway with not a second to spare! I did it! I ran the three miles in 30 minutes in half the allotted weeks! Now what? Where was I going now with all of this? What was the next challenge?

With those questions in mind, I began to prepare myself for Guatemala and the message He had placed inside of me to share. There would be more awaiting me there and when I returned. But I had a new confidence that I could meet the mark whatever the challenge. My confidence was neither in myself or anyone like myself, but in my God and the work that He was doing in me, in the hope that He was renewing in me.

> *Let us hold unswervingly to the hope that we profess, for he who promised is faithful.... So do not throw away your confidence; it will be richly rewarded. You need to persevere so that when you have done the will of God, you will receive what he has promised. (Hebrews 10:23 & 35, NIV)*

Coming into a deeper understanding that His timing was perfect and mine- well- less than perfect, I was more aware of time and its value. Time is one thing that we cannot get back. We have been given a portion, and it is up to us to use it wisely. Our relationship with God will determine how we spend it. Based on that reality, I have maintained a new respect for time. I realize it is not mine to waste. God has invested it in me, and I have an obligation to give Him a good return. With that said, I encourage you to take time seriously. Do not delay in your personal assignments and goals. Your dreams have a purpose, and God wants to implement them in His ultimate plan on this earth. We have to work while it is day, because time is of the essence. It is running out. Night is coming when no one will be able to accomplish what has been given to them to accomplish. Use your time wisely. Do not waste it in prolonged classroom settings. Learn the lessons, and move on to the next level of what God has destined for you.

## *Distance Strategy:*

Be of good courage. I urge you today to throw your confidence on Him. He is the Author and Finisher of your faith. The sooner you believe, the sooner you will achieve. The choice is up to you. In you, lies the key to accomplishing great things. That key is faith. With faith and a clear understanding of the value of time, you will go the distance and fulfill your purpose. The trial will begin to make sense, and the lessons learned will be invaluable. There is no cost too high to pay for this knowledge and this wisdom. Get it at all costs! Remember, it's a good time to be you!

*Wisdom is supreme, therefore get wisdom. Though it cost all you have, get understanding. (Proverbs 4:7, NIV)*

*Part Two:*

*"Get Set!"*

*(Perspiration)*

# Chapter 5

## *The Mountain of Determination*

**The Sovereign Lord is my strength, he makes my feet like the feet of a deer, he enables me to go on the heights.**
**(Habakkuk 3:19, NIV)**

### *Get Over It!*

A little bit of light was beginning to pierce through the darkness that surrounded the atmosphere of our lives. We were able to acquire a contract on the home in which we had invested. In my relief I thought, finally this ordeal was soon to come to an end. We would close on this deal and pay off all debt. We would be out of the mire and back on our way to favor and increase.

With that assumption, I packed my bags and was headed on my once-a-year trip to Guatemala. For the past seven years I had the most wonderful opportunity to visit this beautiful country and the precious people who make it even more special. I considered the cultural town of

Quetzaltenango as a home away from home. Each year I would always return to them with a message to share and a passion to deliver it. They would always greet me with open arms and prepared hearts, ready to receive what God had ordained for them. However, I would always come back home full of insight and understanding as God used them to reveal to me His purpose and plan for my life. I was always receiving more than what I went to give.

On my first visit to Guatemala, I was introduced to a very special lady. She was highly regarded and respected in that town. She was known to have a hot temper at times, and her offspring was even more violent. Her name was, Santa Maria, the largest volcano in Guatemala, and third largest in Central America. Her offspring was Santiaguito, or Little James, the most volatile volcano in Guatemala. The house that I would stay in rested right at her feet. Every day of every visit that volcano would call out my name. I knew at some point in time I was going to have to respond and take the challenge to climb her. Now keep in mind, I was not a mountain climber nor did I really want to be. It was just that I could not escape this urgency to heed the call that I was hearing deep inside of me. I knew an adventure awaited and that the Holy Spirit was drawing me to the heights of a new place in God. I prepared my heart and mind and in February of 2007 accepted that challenge and embarked on yet another adventure of a lifetime.

## The Mountain of Determination

I have learned over the years that mountains are very beneficial and have considerable significance in our lives. Many of us do not like to face them nor have our journeys in life interrupted by them. We see them as intrusive obstacles and with all our finite faith we immediately go into warfare mode and begin to cast them away with our profound spiritual words. Sometimes we even raise the volume of our voices, as if the louder we profess and confess they will bow to our ferocious, intimidating threats. God's Word assures us that we can speak to mountains if we have faith and they can be removed from our paths. That's a really cool concept and I have applied that word in each mountainous situation I have had His consent to encounter. However, in my experiences, I have come to the understanding that some mountains can be moved and others are meant to be climbed. Sometimes we have to exert a little more energy than mere words afford and muster up the necessary faith required to just get over it. Casting away is the easier stratagem to conquering a mountain. It takes greater faith, skill, and endurance to subdue it, climb it, and take dominion of it. In taking dominion, we also acquire a new indisputable authority that is only earned from having gallantly engaged in the unpredictable episodes of the God-ordained exploit.

Psalm 91:11-12 (NIV) relays this message:

> *"For he will command his angels concerning you to guard you in all your ways, they will lift you up in their hands, so that you will not strike your foot against a stone."*

There are some obstacles along the way that we will never see nor encounter. They were present the entire time and were waiting for us to stumble upon them to bring destructive results into our lives- schemes of satan meant for our demise. However, God saw no purpose for them and instructed His angels to lift us over them. Then, there are some obstacles lying in wait where God says, "Okay, angels, surround them. Holy Spirit, walk beside them. Jesus, be their Rear Guard. I'll take the lead. We are walking them through this one. This one we will climb. This one we can use to develop them into the individual we designed from the beginning." It is in those moments, when our faith is being stretched and our trust is being advanced to new levels, that we have no other alternative for survival than to:

> *… dwell in the shelter of the Most High…rest in the shadow of the Almighty…say of the Lord, 'He is my refuge and fortress my God, in whom I trust.' (Psalm 91: 1- 2, NIV)*

## The Mountain of Determination

I was prepared to make my ascent up Santa Maria along with a small group who decided that they would like to accompany. Amongst the eager group was a precious friend that I had made since I had been visiting Guatemala. Her name was Angelica. She and a young boy named Joel proved to be very helpful in my mountain adventure. Another dear friend, Carlos, had organized the excursion and was more or less our tour guide who led us up the gigantic two and half mile high tower of dirt, rock, and molten lava.

Along the path that was created by years of lava flow, I noticed that there were no wild animals on the mountain, just a few nagging flies and bees. Also, I noticed all these beautiful, perfectly straight-lined gardens that had been planted on the side of the rocky terrain. Carlos said that animals did not live on the mountain because they could sense the danger that brewed in its core. However, the volcanic ash provided the most fertile soil, and the gardens produced in lavish abundance.

As he was speaking, I was able to reflect on the heated moments I had experienced in my life. It was during some of the most intense times that I produced the most fruit of God's Spirit. It is amazing how it takes something so extreme to produce strength, beauty, purity, and more of Christ's likeness in us! Nonetheless, it does. Therefore we endure, learn and move on; surprisingly finding ourselves all-the-better for having walked through that fire.

About three minutes into the climb, I realized I had severely underestimated the mountain. My breathing had already become laborious as my heart felt it was beating erratically out of my chest. I had to think for a moment, "This is just the beginning, and I'm already exhausted. But, I'm closer now than I was when I started." Those words became my catch phrase and inspiration as I continued up the steep grassy monster. The higher I climbed, the fewer steps I was able to take before having to stop and catch my breath. I remember challenging myself to take five steps before stopping. I know that five steps doesn't sound like much of a challenge, but believe me when I say those few steps took every bit of determination that was inside of me. My will to take them was great; although, the atmosphere and pressure around me was even greater oppressing each movement of my legs and feet. Occasionally, I could only muster up enough strength to take two or three steps; however, I knew I was closer to the top than I was when I started.

Along the way some people from Norway had passed by. It was at that time, earlier in my journey, that I was making pretty good progress, or so I thought. They had asked if they could walk with me. I was very excited to meet them and was more than agreeable to have them

## The Mountain of Determination

accompany me. I found out that they were experienced climbers and saw Santa Maria as a new dream challenge. They had been studying her and were stoked about finally meeting her. Within just a few minutes of our newly formed partnership, they saw that my pace was getting slower and slower. I guess their youth and adrenaline were fueling their drive. Needless to say, they cordially expressed their pleasure in meeting me and decided to move on full speed ahead. As they left me and my small group behind, little did I realize that would not be my only encounter with them. With only one way up and one way down, our paths would surely cross again.

Some of the members on the excursion team were getting extremely exhausted and needed to cease their climb. Even though I could sense their need, I had to finish this climb. This was not just something to do to say I did it, but it was an assignment. I knew that I had to receive a message. Although, I have to admit at that moment, I could not for the life of me understand why I was on that mountain. All I could focus on was just getting to the top and completing the task. Spiritual thoughts and implications were not even on my mind. I did, however, keep asking God for help to climb it. My constant plea was, "I cannot do this without your help!" Once the others had made their decisions to stop and wait for me to return, I was sent off with great encouragement by Carlos. He instructed Angelica and Joel to continue with me.  He insisted that he would stay with the others and make sure they were safe and taken care of.  I asked him at that point how much farther he thought it was before I reached the top.  I could see it and even felt I could reach out and touch it.  It was one of those "so close and yet so far" moments.  He said I could get there in fifteen minutes.  That sounded encouraging!  I looked at my two companions, and with great effort I proceeded with my ascent.  With all joking aside, that fifteen minutes turned out to be the most physically exhausting one hour and twenty minutes of my life up to that time.  You guessed it!  My interpretation of Carlos' fifteen minutes and his interpretation were quite different.  So for the next one hour and twenty minutes I continued to climb, crawl, and pull my way up to the top of that mountain.

## *Are We There Yet*

"Are we there yet?"  I can recall on several of our family vacations with the kids when they were smaller this infamous question forever resounding from the back seat.  As a child, I never found the back seat accommodations quite the elite, smooth ride either.  Coach is not all that great.  Maybe what made it so unbearable at times was the tight fit or the infrequent snack and bathroom stops or maybe it was the mysterious odors that would loom in the small cramped atmosphere from time to time. Who knows? My mom would always remind us that the fun did not begin once we arrived, but it was during our journey to get there. So, she would then instruct us to sit back and enjoy the ride. If I could have collected a dollar for every time my children asked me, *"Are we there yet?"* Keith and I could have purchased first class airfares for all five of us and arrived at our destination in a much quicker amount of time.

Now, let's bring our focus back to the mountain. I recall at one point losing my footing and my grasp of the tree roots that we were using at that elevation to pull ourselves up. As I began to slide down what had already seemed to be five minutes worth of climbing in about ten seconds, I was caught by a strong arm. It was none other than Angelica. She had been faithfully following behind me as Joel was leading the way in front. I looked at her feet and noticed they were extremely different than mine. She was climbing this monstrosity of a hill in her sandals! God spoke to me at that moment. Finally, I heard something…a word, instructions, an explanation. He told me to look up her name. That was it? I thought, "Is that all you got for me, God, at this moment?" However, He was beginning to show me the significance of it all.

Joel was about thirteen. He could not speak English, and my personal version of the Spanish language was of no use during this time as well. We managed to communicate through smiles and gestures. He would turn around at me and smile, motioning his hand for me to move forward. I would wave mine back asking, "How much farther?" Of course, he did not reply because he had no idea what I was saying. He only smiled and motioned his hand again, as if to say, "Keep it moving!" I could see the top. It seemed close enough to touch, but I still was not there yet! God spoke to me again and said, "You need to look his name up."

Once I had returned home and had access to my computer I did just that. I looked their names up to discover the meaning of my two companions. Angelica, of course, means "angel, messenger." I was reminded of Psalm 91 and how God assures us that he will have his angels watch over us so that we will not stumble or fall. I reflected on how Angelica was right there behind me to catch me when I lost my footing and grasp. Joel means "Yahweh is Lord." I was reminded of Joel leading me. He was amazing. He just kept climbing up with what seemed like the greatest of ease. He would look down at me and just simply smile and motion me forward. There were times I would get frustrated because I wasn't there yet, but his smile was always reassuring to me. Again, I knew I was closer than I was when I started.

Many times as we face the mountains in our lives that are meant to be climbed, we may feel that we are never going to get there- to the top that is. But God always provides His angles to guard us and protect us as He leads us up the ascent to what will become the most memorable moments of our lives- testimonies of what we were able to accomplish with the help of our Lord. These are the signs and wonders that will draw others into a relationship with God. They will see and hear what you have been able to do, and they will desire to do it as well. It's in the Word. Check it out. That's how this thing of advancing the Kingdom works.

I recall crying just minutes away from the top. I again confessed to God that I could not make this climb without His help and strength. It was shortly after, in an unexpected moment that I found myself reaching up one more time to pull my body forward; and, I touched the top! As I pulled myself up and over, I just laid there on the ground with my feet dangling over the edge of the mountain. I was relieved and exhausted. My face was covered in dirt and tears. I had lost my backpack on some other level of the mountain. I had nothing but the jacket I wore around my waist as I began to climb earlier that morning.

Suddenly, I heard hand clapping and cheers, "Go USA! Go USA!" I looked up from kissing the dirt. There before me, sitting on the highest pinnacle of the rocky dome-covered volcano, were the Norwegians. They had been there for a while and were enjoying the warmth of the sun that you felt at that level. They were like witnesses, who had been there and done that. They knew what it took to conquer that mountain. They had already made it and were enjoying the view from "up there." They understood the measure of endurance and could rejoice with me as I made it to the top.

Hebrews 12: 1 encourages us;

> *Therefore, since we are surrounded by such a great cloud of witnesses, let us throw off everything that hinders and the sin that so easily entangles, and let us run with perseverance the race marked out for us. (NIV)*

Sometimes we may feel that no one understands our mountain and the journey that we endure to climb it. But that is just not true. We are surrounded by those who have run this race; walked this path; climbed the heights; and successfully made it to their destinations. They are forever present encouraging us not to stop; to keep moving forward; and to hang in there. They have been there and done that. Now, they are basking in the presence of their reward. And, we will too if we do not give up.

The mountain was surrounded by a skirt of smoke and clouds. Little James had exploded several times during my ascent. He would blow off some smoke and make his roaring noise. It was intimidating at times. I would think, "Maybe I need to get down off this mountain. It's not safe." But, the Lord would speak to me about how the enemy wants to intimidate us during our times of spiritual mountain climbing. He wants us to quit, back down. In order to make us afraid, he begins to blow a lot of smoke and make a lot of noise. That is all! If he can intimidate us with that, then he can achieve the results he desires; such as failure; lack of determination; doubt; anxiety; stress; and even discouragement and loss of hope. We cannot allow his smoke and noise to keep us from reaching our goals and destiny. Our mind-set has to be fixed to the mind of Christ. Many times in the Word, Jesus ignored what satan was saying. He did not give him audience, and neither should we.

Once I had finished pulling myself up and together, I stood on top of the narrow dome. I saw huge boulders on the ground with names and dates inscribed on them. Obviously, they were memorabilia of past climbers who made it to the top. I thought, "Why didn't they tell me people wrote their names on the stones when they arrived? I would have come prepared to do the same thing, but I don't have anything to write with!" The Lord immediately spoke to me, "Why would you want to do that? Why would you want people to see your name? It was just minutes ago you were crying out to Me that you could not do this without Me. You needed My help. It is not in your name that you accomplished this feat, it is in My name. Angela, you will accomplish many other things, but you can never take the credit for them. It is Me that you are to give the honor and glory. You are to draw others to Me and what I can do for them, not to yourself and what you can do."

That was a very profound moment. His words still ring in my ears today. It is not me but Him. I will never be able to accomplish my goals or fulfill my destiny without Him. I will never be able to impact the world around me without Him. I will never be able to take on the next challenge without Him. I am nothing without Him. I live by that knowledge to this day. This was a lesson that I have learned and will always cherish its momentousness in my life.

As I took the short walk to the other side and gazed upon the view all I could see were other mountain peaks bursting through the clouds that surrounded Santa Maria. I could not even see the ground. It was not visible through the thick fluffy layers that encircled her. God began to draw my attention to those massive peaks. He said, "See, there are many more mountains to climb. You can take that one and that one and even that one over there. But first you have to get off of this one." He made it clear to me that in this life we will accomplish many great things. In those moments of victory we can rejoice and celebrate, but we

## The Mountain of Determination

cannot bask in their glory nor remain. We must move on to the next challenge that awaits and calls out. Why? Time is of the essence.

It was in that thought that I was interrupted by Angelica. She was trying to communicate to me that we needed to be making our way back down. I could not understand why. It took five and a half hours to get up here! I've only been here for fifteen minutes. I just got here, and now it's time to go back down? What was up with that? She pointed to her watch and then to the sun. Even though it was still shining brightly, night would soon catch us on the mountain. Being on the mountain in the dark was something that we did not want to happen. It was time to go.

The Lord reminded me of John 9:4,

*As long as it is day, we must do the work of him who sent me. Night is coming, when no one can work. (NIV)*

I realized that there was much to do and little time in which to do it. This is why we cannot bask in our victories. God wants to lead us from victory to victory. In between each victory lies a challenge that must be conquered. This is where many of us fail to be all that we were designed to be. We accomplish one thing and live in that moment for the rest of our lives, basking in yesteryear. But God has planned and purposed for us to accomplish many wonderful things. The work that He has prepared is beyond what we are capable of fathoming. However, God is confident that the work He began in you and in me is good, and He can and will complete it. All we have to do is cooperate with His Spirit and follow His lead. It sounds so simple yet it is so difficult. I encourage you today to allow God to accomplish His great work in you so that He can accomplish even greater works through you.

With that realization, I knew it was time to make our descent. The moment was amazing, and I will never forget it as long as I live. But night would be approaching soon. It gets darker on the mountain quicker due to the trees that cover the light of the sun. My only flashlight was in my backpack somewhere on the mountain. I needed to go.

## The Mountain of Determination

### *Distance Strategy*

What mountain is standing in your way of progress? Maybe it is meant to be climbed rather than cast away. Do not be afraid as you look upon it. Be willing to climb the heights. God is waiting for you to meet Him there. Just like Moses, who was not afraid to climb the mountain to hear from God, so must you be brave and courageous. He is drawing you to a new place with Him and in Him. Take the challenge. It will only better prepare you to go the distance and accomplish the greater things that lay beyond this massive mound! Remember, it's a good time to be you!

> *So do not fear, for I am with you; do not be dismayed, for I am your God. I will strengthen you and help you; I will uphold you with my righteous right hand. (Isaiah 41:10, NIV)*

# Chapter Six

## The Descent of Uncertainty

> Have I not commanded you? Be strong and courageous. Do not be terrified; do not be discouraged, for the Lord your God will be with you wherever you go.
> (Joshua 1:9, NIV)

### Lessons in Humility

There is an arena which many are fearful to enter for within it awaits the sole intent of God's desired purpose- to dispense Christ-like humility. Humility is defined in Webster's Dictionary as the *"quality or condition of being humble; modest opinion or estimate of one's own importance or rank."* God's definition is stated something like this:

> *Who being in very nature God, did not consider equality with God something to be grasped, but made himself nothing, taking the very nature of a servant, and being found in appearance as a man, he humbled himself and became obedient to death- even death on a cross! (Philippians 2:6-8, NIV)*

To be honest, I like the Webster's definition much better. However, I know in order to become the person I was destined to be, it is the second definition that must fulfill its work in me. Even though I have the knowledge of this truth, this is a statement that is much easier to write than to have actually manifested in my life.

A quote by Helen Nielsen that brought laughter to my heart states, "Humility is like underwear; essential, but indecent if it shows." Some are humble and proud of it. Others have humility dowsed upon them through subtle public antics by none other than the great Creator-God Himself. I would like to think of myself as one who was meek and mild, enveloped in an intricate lace of humility. However, I guess in that thought I would be fooling only myself. Abraham Lincoln once said, "What kills a skunk is the publicity it gives itself."

The scent I was giving off must have been highly offensive, for God found it quite necessary to use public antics of humiliation to bring me down from that mountain. I was on my bottom more than my feet while making my descent. The tiny rocks of molten lava gave you the illusion you were on ice. The texture was shiny, smooth, and rather slippery. Each time I would lift one foot to put it in front of the other, I would lose my balance on the slick surface, and both feet would fly out from under me. I would crash to the hard, uneven ground on my bottom.

## The Descent of Uncertainty

The jolt would leave me stunned, and even breathless, as the wind seemed to escape my lungs with each thud. I still bear the marks in my ego from that experience. Nonetheless, in their reminder, I have found purpose.

The descent was a defining moment in my life which over the years has brought more clarity each time I reflect upon it. I was reminded that in order to conquer the other mountains that were shown to me, I must, first, come off of the one I was presently on. I realize that the mountains were only symbolic of the accomplishments I would participate in with God. Some of these accomplishments would be personal goals and visions that God had instilled in me. Others would be the goals and visions that He placed inside of other mountain climbers, who were in need of a guide or mentor to navigate their way and encourage them as they maintained their focus while climbing the heights.

In all truth, I see myself as a Caleb - the one in the Bible who was positively partnered with Joshua. His defining moment was when he chose to be positive and accept a challenge to conquer the land of promise. However, in his zeal, he had to wait forty years for the naysayers to die off. Although we do not hear much from him as it is written in the Word, I'm certain God was performing a work in Caleb also. I would venture to say that over those forty years he became a little more humble, a little wiser, and a little more patient. In due season, God perceived him as ready to take the mountain. So, here he was, forty years older, approximately eighty years old, and very ready, willing, and able to take the new generation up that mountain to take dominion and set up God's Kingdom in the Promised Land. With that being said, I guess I will always be charging or running up and down mountains to advance the Kingdom hopefully a little more humble, a little wiser, and a little more patient.

I am coming into an understanding that it is not the accomplishment itself that bears the reward as much it is the people we motivate and impact along the way. This impact will encourage them to continue their climbs and not give up. They each have the potential to dominate the mountains that God has in their path for a purpose. Some need help in making that domination possible.

Find out what your purpose is on the mountain. Chances are you will encounter one or two on your life's journey. They were not put there to make you afraid or miserable. They were strategically stationed to help define you- to see what you are made of. They were premeditatedly placed to bring humility into your character so that you can release a sweet fragrant, sacrifice in all that you accomplish in your own life as well as in the lives of others.

# The Descent of Uncertainty

## *Taking the Risk*

T. S. Elliot once said, "Only those who risk going too far can possibly find out how far they can go." I have come to firmly believe in that statement. I must admit there is a great fear in taking risks; however, part of the risk is to first conquer the fear. Does that make sense? I will repeat that again...*part of the risk is to first conquer the fear.*

I was halfway down the mountain when Carlos rejoined me. He was making his way up to check on my status and report on the condition of the other climbers. As we were continuing to make our descent he asked me if I had fear. Uncertain of why he was asking in the first place, my initial response was, "No."

He said, "Good, then jump!"

Jump? What did he mean jump? At the end of his command, Carlos took a running leap across a huge chasm that ran through the middle of the mountain. On the other side was ash that looked like black snow. There was no vegetation to be seen. This was obviously the path of the smoke and ash that fumed out of Santa Maria's crusty dome during her active days.

My opened mouth dropped to my chest, and my weakened heart sank to my stomach. I could not believe what he was suggesting that I do! He could not possibly be serious. He reached out his hand and motioned for me to follow. I was stunned and frozen for a moment. My mind was racing with all sorts of scrambled thoughts.

"What if I don't make it? Is this the part where I die? I told him I was not afraid! Surely, I cannot back down now! Am I stupid or what?

Carlos yelled across the deep cavity, "It will save time. It will be quicker, you will see!"

All I could see was a large gaping dark abyss! I could not see the bottom. I did not even know if there was a bottom. What would happen if I fell in? Would I just keep falling to the center of the earth? Would I fall into a pit of all-consuming fire and needless to say, extremely hot lava? My mind was racing and my heart was not too far behind. I could not believe what I was getting ready to do! With a deep breath and a running start sideways on a step mound, I closed my eyes and leaped.

I felt as though I were in slow motion. I thought I would never touch the other side. Maybe I wasn't going to touch the other side. Maybe I was in the hole and was never going to see the light of day again. But with great relief, I felt a thud with -- you guessed it -- my bottom, and I knew I was on solid ground!

I breathed a huge sigh of relief and proceeded to get up and try to stand on my feet. I have to admit, I was shaking all over, and my knees had lost what strength they once had. Carlos motioned for me to stay down. He gave me a huge stick and told me we were going to slide through the ash. This was amazing! I felt like I was sledding through fluffy, thick, white snow. However, it was dirty, ashy, black soot.

We were flying! I felt as though I was going uncontrollably fast. At one point, Carlos, who was leading the way, stopped and turned around to catch me. He said he did that to keep me from flying off the mountain. The terrain was making a curve, and I was about to miss it. Needless to say, I was most grateful for his heroism and strength and his for ability to sense that I was in danger!

When we reached the end of the ash heap I heard one of the other climbers from my group, who had begun the descent while I had continued my ascent, calling my name from above. I looked up and realized, with complete surprise, that I had passed them and was now far ahead of them on the descent. I think we were all stunned by that feat.

As I reflected on that moment, God reiterated to me the importance of our leaps of faith. There will be times in our lives when we think that God has lost His mind! However, it is in that phenomenal, infinite wisdom that He alone possesses that He is able to do exceeding and great things through our exertions of faith. Miracles are a result of this faith. Invincible odds are defied through this faith. Supernatural happenings manifest through this faith. It is through this faith that we grow in our relationship with our Creator as we come to know Him just a little more. This faith requires great risk. It is not for the faint of heart or the doubtful of mind. It is for those who are willing to go too far to see how far they can go.

## *The Next Challenge*

As I was ending my trip in Guatemala and reflecting upon this memorable time in my life, the Lord began to speak to me concerning my recent challenge. I was aware that there was more to this than just running three miles in thirty minutes. I felt I was being prepared for something bigger.

I had opportunity to share with my friends and family in Guatemala the lessons that God had taught me while running. They seemed to receive and were very encouraged by the word that went forth, entering into their ears and settling into their hearts. They embraced the message and declared that they too would be willing to go the distance in the plan that God has prepared for them. I felt I had presented what I was instructed and set out on my way home.

It was while I was on the airplane during my flight back to Charleston, South Carolina that I clearly heard the Lord say, "You will be running a marathon."

## The Descent of Uncertainty

"A marathon?" I replied in shock. Was He serious? Oh, but He was. He told me that I had just begun to learn the meaning of endurance. This lesson was not over but just beginning. Now, you have to understand, up to that point, I had never run any kind of race. I remember as a child trying to run one lap around the baseball field in my Physical Education class. I nearly passed out the first time and had to stop midway. The second day, I did try again and was able to make the lap only to find myself in the nurse's station with a pounding headache. I am not sure if it was from the stress of the run on my young, tender and untrained body or just the stress in my mind from having to prepare myself mentally to finish this lap for a grade. Whatever the reason, I was there with a cold compress on my head lying down on the school infirmary couch. Ah, memories!

Back home in Charleston, Keith was handling our business challenges that continued to mount. Little did I know that the deal we thought we had with the property was no longer a deal, and we were back to square one. This was never going to end, or so it seemed. I realized at this moment that I was running a marathon whether I wanted to or not. I could stop running, but the trial was going to keep moving full speed ahead. The only way to stay focused, sane, fit, and survive, was to be obedient and brace myself for the long haul.

## *Distance Strategy:*

Allow God's processes of humility to produce their good work in your life. Do not defy them or refuse them. They have their purpose, and the results will bring great reward. Do not fear the challenges He presents to you. Each one is to make you stronger in your faith and your ability to make Him great to those who are associated with you. He knows His perfect will for your life. Close your eyes and take a running leap into His opportunities for the miraculous. There are many supernatural moments planned for your life. Defy the odds, and see what is truly in your favor. Remember, it's a good time to be you!

# Chapter Seven

## *Affirming Your Position*

> But he who looks carefully into the faultless law, the [law] of liberty, and is faithful to it and perseveres in looking into it, being not a heedless listener who forgets but an active doer [who obeys], he shall be blessed in his doing (his life of obedience).
>
> **(James 1:25, AMP)**

### *The Announcement*

Upon arriving home, I shared with Keith all the things that I had felt God had spoken to me. He was in total agreement. He knew that God had something extremely relevant that He wanted to impart into our lives. This revelation would not only be for our benefit but it would enhance the life situations of every person with whom we came in contact.

Immediately, Keith began to research marathons. He went on websites and began to study how to prepare oneself physically for such a strenuous race. He ordered a book for non-runners that focused on getting them ready through strict training and scheduled practice runs. Together we were going to do this. It was all or nothing.

In our local congregation, Keith led worship in the early Sunday morning service. Each week he would announce that we were preparing for a marathon. He would give the update of our progress and how many miles we had run that week. I must confess that I was annoyed every time he would share with our friends and family at our worship gatherings. I knew there could be no backing out or partially doing this challenge and still save face. We were really doing this. And for some reason, even though I was preparing, I could not fathom that a marathon was in my very near future!

Once our book arrived in the mail, we set our clocks for the early morning hours to get a start on our training. The book set our distance for us. We would have shorter runs on Wednesdays, Thursdays, and Saturdays. Our longer run for the week would be on Mondays. We were very determined and had each other's company to encourage us and motivate us to reach our weekly goals.

Our diet was even on a strict regimen. We changed bad habits and patterns for more nutritious and healthier ones. It was as if a complete overhaul was taking place in our lives just to prepare for this 26.2 mile race. I am reminded of how God- moments evolve in our earthly existence. We have to prepare for them. We must change our way of thinking from the negative to the positive, from the impossible to the possible and from the fearful to the courageous. We cannot expect to witness the manifestation of God's great accomplishments without having made ourselves ready and able to live them.

Whole wheat products were not exactly my forte, but I grew quite fond of the results in consuming them as they proved most helpful in maintaining good health. I also had to condition myself to eat more fruits and vegetables, and to drink what seemed to be gallons of water. Little did I realize that I had been walking around most of my life as a dehydrated, unnourished participant of the human race. In others words, the changes that did not seem appealing at first were actually making their positive impact on my life. Even during this most difficult time, positive energy was being produced; and, I was in better shape than ever.

When we are actively engaged in God's training program, the same can prove to be true. We may have to do things that we find less than enjoyable, but in the end they really count for 90% of our success. Keith always says, "I do what I don't want to do to become who I want to be." I have learned to appreciate this statement and, these days, find myself quoting him when sharing my experiences.

## *Declaring Our Outcome*

As the distance of our runs increased, the path we chose to take eventually led us to the bank that was ruthlessly on our case concerning the money we owed them. Yes, indeed, we owed them. However, as the saying goes, their efforts amounted to "trying to squeeze blood out of a turnip". You just cannot give what you do not have. It hurt us, especially our pride, to know that we could not pay back the money loaned to us in good faith. Everything we owned in assets was in danger of being confiscated.

Weekly phone calls turned into daily contacts. We could almost set our clock by them. To make a payment on the loans we could pay was a total set-up for humiliation. At our local community credit union we were known as "members with a flag." No longer permitted to make our transactions through the drive-thru, we were instructed that we had to enter the building. Once we were at the desk with the teller, we were made to wait as they made a phone call to their main branch to see if they could accept our payment. After they made the connection with the powers that be, the phone would then be passed to one of us who were asked a series of questions concerning other loans that were in default through our business. After giving them the same answer they were given the prior week, they would then take our payment.

## Affirming Your Position

One day while standing in line awaiting my weekly dose of humiliation, I turned to the person behind me and confessed that I was a "member with a flag;" and, it might take a while for them to take my money. Without hesitation, a look of relief came over the lady's face. This was totally unexpected. I thought she would have been perturbed because her wait was going to be longer than she anticipated. Instead, she began to share with me that she, too, was a "member with a flag"! Go figure, there were more of us out there than I thought.

It seemed that this plague was invading many homes, businesses, and families. I know this may sound insensitive, but I felt so much better knowing we were not the only ones facing such dire straits. I felt strangely comforted and even empowered by the reminder that there is power in numbers. This enlightenment was working for me. I did not feel alone or abnormal at all. In fact, I realized there were even more like us standing in line than like those standing behind the counter with the nagging teller. Others began to join in our conversation, sharing their current situations. It was all the same result caused by the same culprit- an unstable economy.

No one was to blame yet at the same time, we were all to blame. That is life. Things happen; people win and people lose. These are the chances we take in order to pursue our dreams and leave a legacy of a better life for our children and their children. In the process of our labors, decision making, investing, buying and spending, the economy goes up and the economy goes down. It flows on a continuous cycle, and wherever you are in your decisions of the moment will make a lasting impact in your life during each rotation.

Turning our focus back to the running, Keith and I would pass by this bank each day. At first it was very tempting to curse it and say all manner of evil against it (LOL!). We were quickly convicted in our hearts, though, to do just the opposite. So, as we would run through its parking lot, we would begin to bless the very institution that was making our lives miserable. Yes, bless. We would declare it to be fruitful and productive. We would prophesy that this institution was going to, in return, bless us. We came to the understanding that the bank did not have money either. If we cursed it, we would, in the long run, be sealing our doom. This union needed to be blessed so it could once again be productive, fruitful, and abundant in its lending.

We did not stop the blessings there. As we would run through the neighborhoods that surrounded the bank, we spoke blessings and prosperity over the homes and those who resided in them. We blessed each small business and major franchise along the way. This was our community. We were all suffering.

## Affirming Your Position

It was at that time that I experienced an epiphany, an eye-opening reality. Keith and I were not just running for ourselves. We were not just running to maintain sanity during an insane moment in our lives. We were not just preparing for a marathon to say we ran a marathon. We were running for our lives and the lives of all those in our world, the part of the world in which God had positioned us. What an amazing concept! It was not about us! It was about us looking beyond ourselves to see that there were more in the same boat along with us. It was about us rising up to be leaders who would not give up. It was not about our humiliation. It was about us going against the odds and encouraging others to do the same. It was about maintaining hope and, during our own hope-deferring moments, sharing that hope with the hopeless.

## *Distance Strategy:*

There is power in our words. We can speak life or death, good or evil, blessings or curses, positive or negative. It is important that we guard our speech, for many times we have to live by our words. The first place to check is the attitude of the heart. From the heart the mouth will speak. Do not allow the difficulties in life to cause you to become negative or calloused. These are times that God uses to demonstrate His power in your life. Set your sights on all the positive possible outcomes. Begin to speak the will of God into your situation. Even though you may not know what that will is, declare that you are in agreement with it. God knows exactly what He is doing. Remember, it's a good time to be you!

# Chapter Eight

## *Qualifying for the Prize*

Do you not know that in a race all the runners run, but only one gets the prize? Run in such a way as to get the prize. Everyone who competes in the games goes into strict training. They do it to get a crown that will not last; but we do it to get a crown that will last forever. Therefore I do not run like a man running aimlessly; I do not fight like a man beating the air. No, I beat my body and make it my slave so that after I have preached to others, I myself will not be disqualified for the prize.
(1 Corinthians 9:24-27, NIV)

### *Bridging the Gap*

There is a bridge here in Charleston, SC, that is recognized as being the largest of its kind in the United States. It was once named the Cooper River Bridge. Today, with its newer look and grander- built design, we call it the Arthur Ravenel, Jr. Bridge. Once a year, runners from all over the world unite to run across this bridge in a 10K race known as the Cooper River Bridge Run. Some use it as a fund raiser for their favorite charities. Others join in as an opportunity to just have a good time by dressing up in the most ridiculously funny costumes. Some use it as training for participation in future long distance races.

Keith and I would run this bridge during our training for the Myrtle Beach Marathon that was scheduled to take place in February of 2010. It connects the two elite cities of Charleston and Mount Pleasant. Nestled cozily in between is a portion of the Cooper River which flows into the Atlantic Ocean. The expanse of the bridge is approximately 2.5 miles one way. Going and coming would be a nice 5 mile run. It is not unusual to see many other runners, walkers, bikers, and the slow-paced tourists enjoying their activities on the bridge. Its steady incline gives an excellent view of the Charleston Harbor. At its highest peak, one can clearly see over to the beautiful pristine beach of Sullivan's Island, the historical Morris Island Light House, and the many church steeples that tower over the Holy City herself.

While running this majestic elegant bridge, the Lord began to enlighten me in the purpose of my mission on earth. This was not actually just my mission, but the purpose of His Bride in general. He is the bridge that connects two cities; the Kingdom of Darkness and the Kingdom of Light. As His representatives on this earth, we are continually running back and forth on this bridge. We carry with us those who are citizens of the Kingdom of Darkness into a new life and citizenship in the Kingdom of Light. In our run, we cannot be afraid of the darkness. We must go there with the light of Christ in our lives. It is His light which dispels that darkness, allowing those entrapped by it to see truth in the light of God's love. Some are convicted by what they see and willingly follow the path that leads to the Kingdom of Light. Others fear the light and cannot handle the truth and its revelation. Their denial binds them to the false beliefs in their own minds. Sadly, they think there is freedom in the choice they make, yet they remain in bondage to the Kingdom of Darkness and all its perversions.

This bridge has a very special place in my heart. She has been a challenge in reaching her height and distance, but nonetheless, a challenge that I have more than once been willing to meet. Just as she represents Christ to me she also reminds me of His Word, for He is the Word. So when I run on her, I envision myself running on the Word. When I stand on her, I have a visual of myself standing on the Word. The Word is strong, bold, and solid. It can withstand any amount of force or pressure. It cannot only hold me, but everyone else and everything else that finds its way to it. Wow, what a concept!

Some people fear bridges. At one time in my life I had to conquer my fear of this bridge. It was not the height that caused my heart to pound out of my chest, but it was the fact that she arched over a large body of water. As much as I love the beach and all its nautical mysteries, I am not a fan of getting into the water. My fear was water. I would envision myself falling off the bridge through some massive mishap. Spiraling down into the warm Cooper River, I would be swept out into the deep blue sea not being able to get out or survive. That is, of course, if the initial impact did not kill me or if the alligators did not eat me first! I know that sounds crazy, but if you think about it, that would be a frightening thought for you too!

However, while running the bridge, I never focused on my past fear. I realized that the bridge was more than capable of holding me up. She was designed and fashioned in such a way to be able to withstand many forces of nature. So, for the most part, she wasn't going anywhere, and neither was I… except across!

In the same manner, we do not have to fear Christ's ability in our lives to hold us up under extreme duress and intense pressure. We can stand firmly on His Word. The Word is designed and fashioned to make our path solid and our foundation firm. In Him we have nothing to fear. Nothing can harm us from above, from below, or from around. There is no natural or unnatural force that can demolish Him or cause Him to give way. He promises to put His angels in charge of watching over us.

Therefore, we will not fall off or stumble. In fact, the only safe place we have is upon Him!

## *Meeting the Qualifications*

Keith and I had made a determination that we were going to stand upon God's Word and would not waiver. We did not know what was ahead on our path, but our future promised to be bright according to what He was telling us. We had to keep running and believing in what He said. An area that we were forever determined to remain faithful in was our tithes and giving. We had preached of blessings that accompany this principle for years. Now, in a time of dire need, we could not go back on what we knew to be true. We had to remain faithful because He is faithful.

At one time in our lives we had taken a challenge that God had presented to our hearts. He told us that He was going to bring us increase. God wanted us, as an act of faith and trust, to tithe off of what we wanted to make and not just off of what we made. We did just that. And, wouldn't you know it? God in all of His abundance met us there! Go figure! Just like that, He went and did what He said He would do. One should never doubt God at His word. It is what it is.

So, during this moment of what seemed to be desolate lack in our lives, we continued to tithe off of what we had. We did not want be disqualified from the true blessings that were at the end of this race. We knew that He was faithful, and we must be the same in our own measure. After all, we had told others to follow this Word. We could not preach it and then not exemplify it. That would be rather shallow on our part. The god of fear would have been exalted in our lives rather than the one true God in whom we said we put our faith, hope, and trust.

I have to admit, there were times that I would get so angry. After tithes, bills, and other expenses, I would have an amount of $42.00 to feed a household of six for the entire week. This happened around the first of each month as we still tried to make a house payment in hopes of sparing ourselves from what we felt would be the inevitable fate of losing in the end. Nevertheless, with clearness of conscience we could say that we did not go down without a fight. Needless to say, we learned to be very creative with our meals and enjoyed them more than once a week. "Leftovers" became a very common staple meal in our house, and we rather looked forward to them. The only other alternative was fasting. Though it would not have hurt any of us to do that more, it is not something that you really want to do unless you are compelled to do it.

## Qualifying for the Prize

Some would want to argue over the act of tithing and what it really meant back in the day and what they interpret it to mean in our day and age. With respect to all their finite wisdom and knowledge, I am not sharing my experience as to debate it, but to just let you in on the key to our survival during a time of major financial disaster. I encourage you to try it. You will find out what we did. It works. It is a master key, and it will open any door of prosperity, abundance, resource, and supply. If you do not want it, though, give it back; and I will share it with the other persons who are reading this and ready to receive blessings. They will receive their share and more because you opted not to get yours. Just keep doing what you have always been doing if you so desire. However, this is my question to you, "Is it working?"

God's Word and His principles are not open for debate. They are what they are. You either believe them, or you do not. You either put them into action, or you do not. You either reap the rewards for applying them, or you do not. Simply put, that is why some are blessed and others are not.

Tithing is a principle that you can stand firm upon. It will hold you up and sustain you in the most uncertain of times. Even those who are non-believers acknowledge that it is in their giving that they receive more in return. God's principle works no matter who applies it, believers and non-believers alike. So, as a believer, one should practice tithing all the more. As a non-believer, it should persuade you that the rest of the Book is just as effective when you choose to believe.

Month after month, we would barely make it off of what little income came into our home. God was faithful and would make it stretch. We just kept believing and kept running. We were going the distance. We began to think of worst-case scenarios. Just suppose we lost everything. What would happen to us? Where would we go? What would we do?

Keith had always wanted to travel the country in a RV. So, we would think, "Well, we could purchase a RV and set it up at a local camping site. We would have no expenses or ties to anything. The kids are homeschooled, so their studies would not be interrupted. We could travel and see the country like we've always dreamt. As long as we have God and each other, we are going to be just fine! We will bounce back and be all the better for having experienced this." Sounds crazy, right? In all sincerity, we did not care about our habitat. God had promised that we would be fine and that we were not to worry about what we would eat or wear or where we would sleep. His Word told us that. The same Word that told us to tithe and give to Him what belonged to Him.

## Qualifying for the Prize

With that determination in the forefront of our minds, we continued to stand firm on that bridge of faith and truth, also known as His Word. Many things began to happen at an expeditious rate. It seemed as though the tides were beginning to turn. Our mortgage was modified not only once but twice! We got the best interest rate, and our home was spared. The property that we could not sell was finally under contract. On December 31, 2009, we were sitting in a local attorney's office signing closing documents.

We began to call all our creditors and chase them down with cash in hand. They were not quite sure what to do with us, so they settled. All of our debt was cleared for half of what we owed. However, God did not stop there. He made sure that we were not penalized for the remainder. When 2010 tax time arrived we did not owe on what was pardoned and even received a nice return for a year of financial failure. We even woke up one morning $1,100.00 wealthier because Uncle Sam decided that he still had not given us enough in return. While we slept, he deposited a little more into our account.

Overwhelmed is not even the way to begin to describe our emotions at the goodness of our God and His faithfulness. He is not only faithful to you and me, but to Himself. He tells us that He is not a god that would lie to us nor would He be mocked due to His own lack of perfection. In order for God to prove Himself, we have to activate His Word in our lives. In other words, we have to give Him something to work with. He will do what He said He would. Period.

### *It Ain't Over Till It's Over*

After leaving the attorney's office that day, one of the first stops we made was at a local athletic store. I was in dire need of some new running shoes. At this point I had already put over 400 miles on the ones I was wearing. Even though we had this great closing, the trial itself was still opened and in full swing. This was only a small milestone that we had crossed. We had to be faithful to our commitment to run the course and not stop until we had fulfilled our assignment.

On January 1, 2010, Keith and I set out to run our second 14 miles. It was a cold day, and we were ready to get out there and get back to our toasty, warm home. I ran for about two miles and noticed that something was not quite right. My ankles and feet felt like lead; and, with every thud on the cement sidewalk I had excruciating pain. It was in mid-run that I had to stop. Keith was farther ahead of me than usual. He had not noticed that I was running at a much slower pace.

I called out to him, and he turned back to check on me. I explained to him what was happening. It just so happened that his parents were visiting with us and were at our house. I called on my phone for Dallas, Keith's dad, to come and get me. For some reason I was very emotional and began to cry. I knew this was not good. Keith tried to encourage me and told me not to cry, but it was so hard to stop. I could not imagine why I was not able to run. Within a very short amount of time, Dallas had me back at the house with ice packs on my ankles.

Due to much insistence from well-meaning friends and supporters of our run, I made an appointment to see a doctor. I was not happy with the results. I was diagnosed with stress fractures on both ankles. I was told to stay off my feet for a month. I had permission to go from the bed to the couch to the bathroom and back to bed, nothing more. When I wanted to argue with that treatment, I was told it was better than having to stay off my feet for six months and chancing the possibility of never running again. Considering the alternative they so matter-of-factly shared with me, I opted to follow the instructions of the first treatment plan.

I sat for an entire month. I could not imagine why God would not have wanted me to run the race in February in Myrtle Beach. This was not making sense to me. Discouragement tried to set in. However, I encouraged myself with, you guessed it, His Word. I knew that I had heard from God. I was going to run a marathon, maybe not Myrtle Beach, but I would run a marathon.

While I was off my feet I received a flyer in the mail. It was for a group of runners that ran for a cause. In this case it was for leukemia and lymphoma. They were trained by expert running coaches and raised funds in order to be able to participate. One of the marathons listed was scheduled for June of that year, 2010, in San Diego, California. I remember the Lord speaking so clearly to me, "This is your race. This is the marathon I am preparing you for. I am sending you to be trained by expert runners. You will focus on the needs of others. There is more I will teach you during this chapter of your life. I will heal you and give you opportunity to run. Will you go the distance?" Once again, my answer to Him was, "Yes, I will go the distance."

I realized that it was not over. I still had more to experience as He accomplished great feats in my life. It seemed as though I would never heal. I was sent to physical therapy. The therapist asked me if I had prepared myself for the thought of never being able to run this race. My response was, "No, I'm not there yet." I was sent to another doctor who prescribed orthotics for my running shoes. These seemed to help tremendously. The Lord was showing me once again that He was in control. He was providing me with the equipment that I needed to be able to successfully complete this mission.

It was at the end of my recovery and the Myrtle Beach marathon was already being threatened by a surprising forecast of snow. Now, mind you, marathons are not canceled, especially due to inclement weather. They go on just like the mail still runs. However, in the South, we are not accustomed nor prepared to handle snowstorms. In a last minute decision, the "Powers that Be" called the marathon off. Talk about a total upset! Avid runners, who had traveled from all over the world and were already secure in their hotels, could not believe what they were hearing. This was totally unheard of.

The Lord showed me once again, that He was in control. This was definitely not my race. I needed this time of rest and recovery because my race was still ahead. I was getting stronger each day and the anticipation of getting back on my feet was unbearable. All I could do to stay focused and reassured was to tell myself, "It ain't over till it's over."

## *Distance Strategy:*

Many things will try to stop you. Discouragement is one of them. Always maintain your faith by putting your hope in the truth of God's Word. Believe me when I say, "It will not fail you." If you remain in hope you will get what you are in need of. Not only that, but you will qualify for the even greater events in which He wants to involve you. So, stand firm in your faith. Do not be afraid and just believe. He is in control. Remember, it's a good time to be you!

*Part Three:*

*"GO!"*

*(Participation)*

# Chapter Nine

## *Preparing to Participate*

**If we endure, we will also reign with him.**

(2 Timothy 2:12a, NIV)

### *To Be, or Not To Be?*

Have you ever wondered what all this suffering was about when it comes to being like Christ? Well, I have. I never found it appealing or something that I wanted to embrace on a regular basis. There were times when I would suffer and the mere meager thought would come to me, "Well, I am going through this for the sake of others."

Come now, I know that a few of you out there have experienced that martyr syndrome before. You know the one where you pay the price for others to come to know Christ, or receive their healing or be delivered from similar bondages that you have experienced. Well, please allow me to share with you what God once shared with me. It was a lesson that to this day is firmly planted in my soul. I will NEVER forget it!

I was the type of person who would do anything for anybody. I had a tremendous codependency issue and my temperament allowed me to be a stepping stone for many. In the process of trying to please people, I also was desperate for God to find pleasure in all that I did. I wanted everyone to know Him as I did and would do anything to make that happen. Even though I would never admit it, I was driven by the "works" thing; trying to find acceptance through working myself nearly to death!

At the time, the church we still attend was conducting quarterly conferences called Encounters. These conferences were designed to help an individual understand in the simplest of explanations the love that God has for us all. In them, the person would discover the beauty inside of themselves and the true heart that Father God has towards them. Needless to say, I would invite as many people as I could. Then, I would volunteer not only to pick them up, but I would also pay their way! All in an effort to ensure that they would attend. You can only imagine how expensive this strategy was becoming.

In order to keep up the standard that I had already set and be fair to all by paying for all, I came up with several ideas for fund raising. I

## Preparing to Participate

would collect donations from others who I knew had the pocket change to spare. I would have bake sales. I even pawned some of my most treasured pieces of jewelry. Then one day, I had this marvelous idea, the idea to top all other ideas. I would sell my blood! Yes, you read it right. I would sell my blood.

I heard an advertisement on the radio about selling your plasma for money at the local plasma center. How cool was that? I could earn money to get these people to the Encounter. My blood could pay for them all! What a concept! What an idea! What a fool was I!

Don't get me wrong. There is nothing abnormal about the concept of selling plasma. It is much needed and is used for a wonderful cause. Medicines, vaccinations and other research have advanced through the harvesting of plasma. It is just that my motivation and intentions were not quite in sync with God's Word or His purpose. It was not the fact that I was doing it. It was the "why" behind my doing it.

I began selling my plasma at the local laboratory. I could get top dollar for mine because I had the hepatitis B series of vaccines. I was required to have this vaccination when I worked in the medical field. The center would pay $25 for a weekly donation. It would then pay an additional $45 for a second donation within the same week. This totaled to $70.00 a week. That would allow one person entry at the Encounter.

I would go twice a week.... religiously! This process required about an hour per visit, two hours if you counted my travel time to the center and back, I would lie back in a comfortable chair, but extremely cold room, and squeeze this little ball. I would watch my blood leave my body, flow through a tube and enter into a machine which held a little glass bulb. My blood would go inside this bulb. There it would be separated into blood cells and blood fluid or plasma. The fluid would flow into a different tube which ended in a small bag. The cells would follow the direction of another tube that ended with a needle inserted into my arm. So, they would take the fluid and give back the cells. What I was seeing at the other end of the needle were all the souls that I would impact for the cause of Christ.

Hello! It is time to be awakened. One day while sitting and pumping, I recall feeling extremely tired. I was so ready to stop doing this blood thing, but too proud to admit it. If I quit, what would happen to all those souls out there who needed to encounter Christ? I was feeling really guilty about my torn thoughts. But, suddenly, I had an epiphany!

I was in deep conversation with God when I heard myself say, "My blood is not sufficient to save these people, only Your blood is." Immediately, the machine began to sound off an alarm. The nurse came running into the lab. She frantically worked with all the buttons and gadgets on the outer box. I looked over the side of my chair and saw my blood spilling on the floor. What was happening? Without hesitation, the nurse removed the needle from my arm and wrapped it in a bandage. She was very apologetic as she cleaned up the pool of spilt blood. Once she finished, she informed me that I would not be able to come back for a while. For some unknown reason, the glass bulb inside the machine that held my blood burst making it impossible for the blood cells to reenter my body. She said it was as if I had donated blood. I would have to wait at least eight weeks before returning.

I knew what happened. This was my wake up call. I was not going back. I had finally gotten it! It was not my blood or my suffering that was sufficient for others; it was Christ's. I will never suffer for the sake of others. Christ already did that on the cross. How could I, or anyone else, possibly top that? What was I thinking? My tests will only enlighten others as I share my testimonies. That's all. It will not save them, deliver them, nor heal them.

So, why suffer? If Christ did it all then why is it necessary that we suffer? It is so that we can qualify to participate in what He was already doing, with or without us. Believe it or not, the blood of Jesus has been saving souls and changing lives for centuries. He was already accomplishing great results before you or I ever entered the world. Go figure!

Our personal suffering, however, produces perseverance; and, perseverance produces hope. We must have hope if we are going to work with God. He does not want a bunch of hopeless people doing His work. It just will not happen. Good intentions fail, kind words fade, but hope does not fail us. James 1: 12 tells us,

*Blessed is the man who preservers under trial, because when he has stood the test, he will receive the crown of life that God has promised to those who love him. (NIV)*

It is only by placing our hope in Christ Jesus that we are able to do anything. We can beat impossible odds. We can go against the majority and win. We can be a light in the darkness.

With hope we can be. We can be participants with Christ. We can be included in His beautiful bride who shines. We can be trusted with the most valuable treasure known to God, mankind. We can be history makers and make His mark in our day and time on the face of the earth. Wow, there is so much to be said about hope!

## Preparing to Participate

*Let us hold unswervingly to the hope we profess, for he who promised is faithful. (Hebrews 10:23, NIV)*

I encourage you today; make the right choice. Come to the understanding that it is only He Who is sufficient. He has already done all it takes for the work to be completed. You cannot save souls, nor can you direct their destiny. However, you can participate in what God is doing to complete His work in them. Now, with all that pressure taken off of you, the choice should be easy. The choice is yours: to be or not to be.

### *Joining a Team*

Keith and I were very excited to join the league of marathon runners. Finally, we were a part of a team, had a coach that could instruct us, and participated in training that would prove priceless in the end. Our training group runs were on Tuesday evenings. No matter where we ran or what time of the day we ran, I was always found at the end of the line or the caboose. I was still recovering from the injury, and was not born to run. Both of these facts were contributing factors in my less than excessive need for speed. Regardless of my lower than standard pace, I never gave up on the run and always finished my course.

I recall there were times the others would be passing me in the cars waving goodbye, as I was half-way back to the gym where we met for training. Keith could have easily kept up with the best of them; however, always being considerate of me, he would maintain my unchangeable pace. He was a true partner to the highest degree.

Being a part of a team opened up many opportunities for us to meet new people. This was something that we thoroughly enjoyed. We got to know them and learn a little about their lives. We found their experiences in life to be very inspiring as we developed relationships. They shared their stories of how they became involved in running for the organization that raised money for leukemia and lymphoma. Many had lost loved ones to the disease of cancer. Some just wanted to participate in a productive run. Others were survivors of cancer and felt empowered with each race they entered to fight against it. Wow, what heroes!

Some of them still had fresh wounds from the battles. Keith and I took the opportunity to reach out to them during times of warming up, stretching or even at the social events that were hosted by the running coach. We felt a certain draw to them and their need. I could imagine this was what Jesus did when He walked the earth. He hung out where the people were. He became a part of them, and their needs were His opportunity to demonstrate the unconditional love of the Father.

## Preparing to Participate

Tuesday evenings became our ministry. We would have rather been there than in a Sunday worship service or Wednesday evening meeting. It just felt right.

Many times as believers, our ideas and concepts of ministry are far from God's. We think we have to bring everyone to the church building to have "church" for it to really count as ministry. These are the traditions of religious methodology. Pardon me for being so abrupt, but that's just stupid. If you think like that, please don't any more. Grab hold of this concept: ministry is wherever you are at any time and in any way. Jesus never hung out in the synagogues. When He was present, he was challenging the hypocrites who made that building their main headquarters and dwelling place. He spent most of His time in the streets with the people, the very ones whom the religious would not accept or allow entrance into their beloved sanctuaries. Being laced with a slight hint of rebel nature, this is what I most admire about Jesus. He hated religion. Now, I don't feel so bad for sharing in His sentiments. It is my personal desire to become more like Him in that area.

The team became our family. We shared a common bond and a common spirit. Together we were working towards the same goal, the same prize. We wanted to finish what we had started. We did not want to see anyone not make it. Continually, we would encourage each other to keep running and not give up the training. Love was immediately demonstrated and felt; a love for the purpose and a love for each other.

This reminded me of what the Kingdom of God is all about, LOVE. 1 Corinthians 13:13 shares,

> *And now these three remain: faith, hope, and love. But the greatest of these is love. (NIV)*

So many times we get caught up in our own worlds' and ideas of how to live in the Kingdom. Some are just trying to survive. Others feel it is their duty to judge who can enter and who cannot. And still others do not believe in it at all. To be honest, I can't blame the latter when I compare them to the first two.

Jesus was all about love and passion. He loved the sinner and hated the sin. He could distinguish satan from the individual. He embraced the hopeless and gave them a reason for living. He healed the sick and delivered the oppressed and possessed. He shared the principles of the Kingdom in a language they could understand. His simplicity and approachability was a magnet for those who so desperately needed Him.

## Preparing to Participate

He challenged those who wanted to follow Him by bringing it to their attention that He had no place to live or sleep. For all purposes, He considered Himself homeless and liked it. He was out and about. He did not want to be confined to one place or be put in a box, so to speak. Sometimes He did not wash his hands before He ate, and He picked corn on the Sabbath. He ate with sinners and allowed those who were considered less-than and of ill-repute to touch Him. His methods were questioned, and His identity was debated. But one thing remained, He was who He was- Love.

As followers of this disputable Jesus, who are we really? Are we people who get caught up in the cares of this world, or are we people who realize this world is not even our home? Are we people who can be easily swayed by what others think of us, or are we people who are sure of our mission in life and only care what the One who sent us thinks? Are we people who are bound by religiosity, or are we bound to the heart of God and the mind of Christ? These are some questions that we have to know the answers to. We have to be convinced in who we are and Whose we are. We cannot vacillate; we have to know.

There is a world hurting and suffering. There is a team that God is putting together to serve a common purpose- to reach them with His love. The qualifications require that we have more of Him in our lives and less of ourselves. The way to meet those qualifications is to meet Him. We must come to a realization of who God is and who we are not. It is His blood and His love alone that empowers us with the ability to participate with Him in His work in the lives of others. Without His virtues we are nothing and can do nothing. With them, we can do all things!

## *Distance Strategy:*

**There are many things that can hinder us from participating in God's work. These hindrances do not have to remain. In order to share God's love, we must first experience it. I encourage you to embrace God and allow His love to flow into those areas that bring about distractions, pain, insecurity, doubt, and fear. Involving yourself in the lives of others as Christ's representative is a most rewarding life. It is one of highest honors as God can entrust you with what is most precious to Him- the human soul. Do not allow religious ideas and concepts to hinder your purpose. Ask God in all His love to remove these things from your heart. In discovering the power of His love in your own life, you will be set free TO BE! Remember, it's a good time to be you!**

# Chapter Ten

## Give Me This Mountain

Now give me this hill country that the Lord promised me that day....
(Joshua 14: 12, NIV)

### California or Bust

The time of recovery for the Henderson family was one of great adventure, direction, and focus. During a time when we could have raised funds for ourselves, here we were raising $5,800.00 for leukemia and lymphoma. I must say our creativity in sales truly emerged from a war-weary business sense.

We opted to flip cars as a means to generate the funds for our mission. The first car we sold was our own which was paid in full. From there we proceeded to go to the car auction and purchase vehicles that we could refurbish at minimal cost and then resell. This was a great success.

With that endeavor and the personal financial contributions of a few friends and family, we had met our goal.

As we conquered in this area, we also began to receive strategy on how to conquer the financial goals that we had set for ourselves. We used the same method. We became experts in the field and flipped whatever we could. Little by little we began to see an increase in the storehouse of our limited supply.

God was teaching us to look beyond ourselves and have a deeper sense of compassion for the needs of others. As we truly began to seek after His kingdom and His righteousness, all the things we had need of were brought to us. One open door led to another. What we thought were random acquaintances became priceless connections. I always thought of myself as a people person and loved everyone I ever met. However, through all of this I learned a greater appreciation for people. They can be our most valuable resource; what beautiful treasures reside in each one. I began to see people in a different light. Their pain pierced my newly molded heart. Their stories brought tears to my refocused eyes. My in-tuned ears could actually hear what was not being said. The Holy Spirit had found a deeper habitat in my very soul. There was a little more of Him and a little less of me operating in the temple of my body.

## Give Me This Mountain

As we began to conduct more research on the running trail for our San Diego encounter we noticed that the path was extremely hilly. This came as a surprise to us; and, to be quite honest, it was rather overwhelming. We live in what is affectionately called the "low country" of South Carolina. There are no hills only flatlands. The only hill we had to practice on was the Arthur Ravenel, Jr. Bridge that extended over the Cooper River and connected downtown Charleston to the city of Mount Pleasant. Every time we ran that bridge, I would reflect on my mountain climb. I was rather intrigued by conquering the heights and was willing to take on the challenges that came with that endeavor. However, when I gazed upon the map of our running path, I saw inclines that would last seven miles or more. The downhill run looked rather easy, but once you came down, you would have to go back up.

Feeling a little intimidated at what we had discovered we decided to run that bridge as much as possible in preparation for what awaited us. I enjoyed conquering the Mount Pleasant side of the bridge first. Even though it was steeper and a monster to behold, once you were on top and reached the first tower, it was downhill all the way to Charleston. This was a nice run and allowed me time to catch my breath. Coming back was a great challenge. It was a steady incline for about a mile-and-a-half. This was a place where I would see many runners grow weary. You could see the strain on their faces. You could see the drops of sweat they left on the concrete of the bridge. This ascent was requiring a lot from them. The force of gravity was not on their side but rather opposed them as they strained towards the peaks that rose ahead. However, in spite of the difficulty, I would witness them as they victoriously made it to the top and ran with accelerated speed down the other side.

In light of this visual, I saw myself and Keith and the difficulty we had just passed through. I was able to compare our ascending efforts to the conquest of that bridge and its challenges. I could see how the circumstances wanted to overpower us through their intimidation. I understood how imperative it was to stay focused and not lose sight of the mark. I felt the strain in my mind, emotions, and body. I saw the opposition and had to push against the oppression, depression, and lies that it wanted to use to bring confusion into my heart and mind. I had a choice to either overcome it or allow it to overcome me. Now, standing in the reflection of my choice, I was taking on another challenge that would actually enhance the quality of life for someone else. Wow, what an honor!

### *Taking the Hills*

As I am writing this chapter, I just received a text message from my friend, Tina, who I had coffee with the day before. In her message she writes,

## Give Me This Mountain

*"Good morning, I just wanted to let you know that I am very excited to go on the journey and especially having you as my mentor. I am so thankful that you came into my life at a time when I was desperate for answers to get out of the valley I was in. The Lord put you in my life and I'm glad I chose to keep you there. I love you, Ms. Angela, and thank you for loving me."*

This is what it is all about! It is not about me or the suffering I have experienced. I need not grieve over my sacrifices but rather rejoice that they have allowed me to qualify to participate with God in what He is doing in the life of another.

Caleb has always been an inspiration to me. As I read his life's story in the Bible, I see that he is a faithful friend and spy-companion of Joshua. Together they gave a positive report of the Promised Land. They saw beyond what the other ten spies had reported. As the others were sharing their horror stories of the giants that dwelled in the land, Caleb and Joshua were testifying of gigantic fruit that was growing in the land. In spite of the inhabitants, Joshua and Caleb knew they could take it. God said it was theirs, and that was enough to go for it. However, the people chose not to receive the positive report and allowed the negative report to influence their decision not to go and possess it.

Standing in the reflection of their choice, they were penalized. No one of that generation would be able to enter the Land of Promise, that is, except for Joshua and Caleb. They had to wait while the others died. In the meantime a new generation was rising. They had only heard the tales but had never seen the land of controversy. But when the time came to take it again this was Caleb's response:

*Now, then, just as the Lord promised, he has kept me alive for forty-five years since the time he said this to Moses, while Israel moved about in the desert. So here I am today, eight-five years old. I am still as strong today as the day Moses sent me out; I'm just as vigorous to go out to battle now as I was then. Now give me this hill country that the Lord promised me that day. (Joshua 14:10-12, NIV)*

Caleb was not a "quitter." He had believed in what God said was his, and he wanted it. There were others who were now a part of his life who had never been up that mountain. But just the same, they desired to see the Land of Promise and all its treasures and needed him to lead them. Caleb never gave up on what God told him he could have. This should be inspirational to all of us. Never give up on God's word in your life. No matter how long the wait has been or how high the climb do not quit. Remain positive and faithful in your belief in what He has promised you.

The Land of Promise was divided among all the tribes of Israel. Believe it or not, there were some who just stood there looking at their territory but never put the first foot forward to go and take it. They were overwhelmed at the challenge and all the imaginations of the "what ifs" that clouded their senses. Joshua encouraged them to go; instead, they just stood and looked at the promise.

God is not going to do for us what He expects us to do for ourselves. He has made the promise to us. He even gave us His word that His presence will go with us. But it is up to us to go. We have to advance towards the promises and take hold of them.

*Let us hold unswervingly to the hope we profess, for he who promised is faithful. (Hebrews 10:23, NIV)*

We have to take the steps of faith in the confidence that we have placed in Him.

*So do not throw away your confidence; it will be richly rewarded. You need to persevere so that when you have done the will of God, you will receive what he has promised. (Hebrews 10:35, NIV)*

What is the will of God? The will of God is that you walk in confidence and persevere. Take the mountain. Possess the territory that God has promised you. Do not allow distractions and intimidations to stand in your way of having what God said you could have. Do not keep yourself from being effective in helping others reach their heights. Simply put, when we take the initiative and make the first positive move towards the promise, God will meet us and go with us.

### *Joining the Rank of Champions*

Arriving in San Diego was a great experience. Our plane was packed with passengers who were on the same mission as us. The next evening after we landed, we were escorted to a convention center where there was a huge pasta dinner gathering. As we were taking the escalator to the fourth floor, you could hear a great sound of fanfare with all the bells and whistles.

In my mind's eye I could see all the runners gathered and providing this warm welcome for the cancer patients, who would be our honored guests. However, I was humbly surprised when I reached the top of the stairs to discover this fanfare was not created by the runners but for us. In actuality it was the hundreds of cancer patients who had gathered together to greet the runners with such intense passion and gratitude. I was overwhelmed with this reality and could hardly see where I was walking for the tears that were welling up in my eyes.

As we sat through dinner, one by one patients, family members and friends walked to the podium and shared their stories of their personal battles with the cancer. It was touching to see the photos and videos that they displayed of precious memories. This was a very intimate moment being shared with perfect strangers. Or, were we? Yes, it is true that we did not know each other. However, we had something in common- the love for life and the determination to fight for it.

I was reminded of the Kingdom of Light and how it flows with this same love and abundant acceptance. Even though we may not know each other on a personal level, as believers we have a common bond. We love eternal life and desire to share the mystery of achieving it with all. We are surrounded by a cloud of witnesses who have gone on before us and are now cheering us on. I can just imagine them blowing their whistles, ringing their bells, clapping their hands, and shouting out cheers and accolades as we who remain on earth are still running our course and participating in sharing the gift of life.

The author of Hebrews encourages us,

> *Therefore, since we are surrounded by such a great cloud of witnesses, let us throw off everything that hinders and the sin that so easily entangles, and let us run with perseverance the race marked out for us. Let us fix our eyes on Jesus, the author and perfecter of our faith, who for the joy set before him endured the cross, scorning its shame, and sat down at the right hand of the throne of God. Consider him who endured such opposition from sinful men, so that you will not grow weary and lose heart. (Hebrews 12:1-3, NIV)*

I personally find great encouragement in this passage of scripture. Nothing I do will surpass what Christ did for me on the cross. However, with pleasure I will do all that I can do to share what He did not only in my words but also in my actions. I desire to demonstrate His love, compassion, and passion. As the saying goes, "Actions speak louder than words." This is so true. I do not just want to talk about it, but I want to live it, be it, and show it! Too often, as believers, we fail to do the latter. In our negligence, many have not experienced the true love and mercy of a just God. They are still thirsty and hungry for more than what they have, and what we have offered has not been sufficient.

There is no better time than the present to stop what we may have been doing wrong and begin to represent Him in the right way. We need to evaluate what we have been offering the world. Would they be any better if they partook of what we have offered them? Or, worse, would they remain the same?

I must allow His faith to be made perfect in me. In doing so, I become a witness of His goodness. I can be strong and not grow weary. I can finish my course and encourage others to do the same. I can get past myself and see the needs of others as they are revealed through the light of the Spirit. I take my honored position among the unstoppable team of champions!

## *Distance Strategy:*

**Do not be overwhelmed by the mountains that face you. Within them your promises await. Take the hills, and lead others up to conquer as well. Set your mind on the prize and your eyes on the mark. Do not let anything or anyone hinder you from reaching that goal. Write it down on paper, and evaluate your progress every day. God will deposit His resources and opportunities into an action**

plan. If you are doing nothing, then He will do nothing. So, get going and get active. Be determined to possess the promise that He has spoken to you. Remember, it's a good time to be you!

# Chapter Eleven

## *Kicking Satan's Ass*

**The God of peace will soon crush Satan under your feet.
The grace of our Lord Jesus be with you.
(Romans 16:20, NIV)**

### *Survival of the Determined*

I have probably offended some of your religious ideology by now. Well, all I can say is, "GOOD!" Religion has a tendency to keep us ignorant of the reality that is truly taking place around us. It will cause us to judge some of the most stupid and insignificant things. It will keep us distracted and preoccupied with matters that do not even interest the heart of God and cause us to miss opportunity to partake in His true righteousness. With that being said, I make no apologies for the title of this chapter. I hope that you will allow the message to sink into your heart and join me in kicking Satan's ass.

Too many times we as believers, followers of Christ, or disciples, allow ourselves to become victims of our circumstances. We take on the martyr mentality and begin to chant the "why me's," as though we pay some enormous price to bear the cross that we think we bear. When in reality we have been given an opportunity, afforded a privilege, and marked for success to demonstrate the characteristics of the One in Whom we say we believe, follow and are called disciples. When our words and self-proclaimed titles are put to the test, many times we find ourselves wanting and not quite measuring up to the standards we profess.

This is as far as religion will take us; mere words. It has no substance, no power, and no ability to survive in the heated demonstrations of divine activity in our lives. Religion, when put to the test of fire, will burn to ash just like any other flammable substance. Yes, flammable. Religion is flammable. In serving it we will seal our hellish doom, just like any other sinful choice or desire that we do not bring under the submission of Christ's blood and God's work in our lives.

Satan loves to play games with our professions of faith and will stop at nothing to make fools of us all. He wants the world to see our God to be as weak as our religious walk. In that, we truly have nothing different to offer the world. Those who are suffering and in need of divine intervention in their lives see the religious in worse condition than themselves. Who needs that? So what are we offering? Drama, trauma, disorder, and confusion seem to be the most popular dishes inscribed on the menus of many Christian lives. With that being the selection to choose from, a non-believer would have a better chance at leaving well enough alone in their own carnal nature.

So, what am I saying? I am saying that in order to survive this race we have to be determined to take hold of something that has more substance than mere religious beliefs, ideas, traditions, and limited knowledge. We need to embrace a relationship with Christ and put into practice the freedoms that relationship affords. One freedom is that of taking authority over the accuser and the oppressor of our faith- none other than satan himself!

When we prepared for the longer distances in our running scheduled, Keith and I would fill up the night before on carbohydrates. Our favorite place was the little doughnut shop about three miles from our house. Every Sunday evening we would place our order for a dozen donuts and get a dozen free! It was a "sugar land" delight! Now, if one wanted to lose weight, they would usually go on a strict diet that would eliminate, or at least strictly limit, the amount of carbohydrate consumption. However, our goal was not to lose weight, even though that was a by-product of our running. Our goal was to have fuel and energy to finish the long-distance run ahead of us.

As God is sending you out to truly make a difference in this world of darkness and shine brightly as a representative of the Kingdom of Light, He may require you to say things or partake in activities, ideas, and ways that will abrasively go against the grain of your religious concepts. This is where you as a believer have to work out your salvation with fear and trembling while making your calling and purpose sure in Christ.

Even Jesus went against religious order and law to relate to the people and step into their world. As He engaged in their daily activities, celebrated festivities, and participated in moments of decision, He gained authority to speak into their lives a peace that helped them to look beyond their current circumstances and see a brighter future in the light of the Father's love. Now, that same ability has been granted to us as His disciples. How are we doing with that? Have we allowed ourselves to go back to a form of religion that separates us once again from the very ones that the cross of Christ helped to bridge the gap? Are we too weak and too afraid of being contaminated so that we walk on the other side of the road and make the foolish decision not to waste our time in helping those who have been beaten, stripped, robbed, and left for dead by the enemy of their true destiny? What are we doing?

The madness of just trying to get myself into heaven has got to stop! We must take others into consideration and operate in the confidence that Jesus offers us daily. As we allow His work to be completed in our lives our confidence level begins to rise. This allowance is manifested by spending time with Him through the reading of His Word, having continual conversation with Him, and emulating what we have read about Him. In other words, we have to put what we know into practice. Our determination of becoming more like Him will be a key to our survival.

I witnessed many who started their marathon training quit. They did not feel they could meet the required challenges of raising the funds, participating in the meetings, and running the miles. It sounded like a good idea at the time, and for a while they were really stoked. But as it got a little harder and more demanding of time, energy, and resources, they just could not give what was necessary in order to succeed. They could not give determination. They could not give it their all, and their all was what was required.

In our run for the Kingdom we have to give it our all or nothing. Why? Because He wants to replace it with all that He has to offer. He wants to activate His authority in our lives so satan will quiver as we walk into a situation in which he thought he was in control. He screams at the presence of God and the light that accompanies it. He steps back and bows to the name of Jesus, a name he knows all too well. This is the authority that God desires us to have operating in our lives. It only comes through a determination to be less like ourselves and more like Him.

## *The Thirteenth Mile*

The race had begun, and we were into it with full speed ahead. The first six miles was a curvy downhill route. It was a wonderful, exhilarating start! However, the next seven miles became a grueling uphill climb that tested even the most seasoned runner's abilities.

I remembered the instructions of a dear friend, Patricia, as I was in the Atlanta airport en route to San Diego for the race. She was determined to reach me before running the race. She said that God told her she needed to call me and share with me a strategy for taking on the hills that I was about to encounter. Being a runner from Mexico herself, she said at one time she had to run hills on a regular basis. The way to conquer them was to climb them. She instructed me to drop my shoulders, raise my knees, lower my head, and envision myself climbing stairs. With that in mind, I began to climb a seven-mile-high flight of stairs on the hilly streets of San Diego.

Crowds were positioned along the roadside. They were cheering us on and congratulating us on our progress. Cancer patients would shout through megaphones, *"Thank you for what you are doing. Because of your sacrifice I have an opportunity to live!"* Talk about inspiration! There was no stopping, no turning back. I was in a race with a purpose. I had to fulfill that purpose. I was closer to my destination than when I started. I was determined to make it. I was determined to fulfill my assignment. I was determined to make a difference.

With that determination, yet running a little slower, I topped the steepest hill we would run, the thirteenth mile. Ah, I was halfway there! Naturally, thoughts began to flood my mind. "Is it realistic for me, a first-time marathon runner, to think I could actually finish this race?" I had never run a race before in my life! And of all races, I had to start by running a marathon, 26.2 miles! It was at that moment I noticed a sign posted on the left side of the road. When I saw it I began to laugh. It said,

***"Your feet are hurting right about now because you're kicking cancer's ass!"***

Never had a truer statement been made at that point! To me that was the most profound observation during my run. Yes, I was hurting. Yes, I did have thoughts of not being able to make it. Yes, my body felt like it was shutting down. But, I was making progress! I was not defeated! The race was not over! I was still running! And with that encouragement and motivation, I continued to run.

The tormenting thoughts of quitting ceased with the peace that flooded my heart. To begin with I was very content in my purpose for embarking on this adventure. I was going to be counted among the 1% of individuals who actually accomplished the feat of running a marathon. It wasn't just that satisfaction alone, but it was in knowing that I was actually helping to defeat an illness that had claimed millions of lives throughout time. Could it be that I am a part of a team that will actually see this villain of health and happiness annihilated? I am convinced that my contribution mattered!

So, I am also convinced that my contribution to the advancement of the Kingdom of Heaven on this earth matters. Many times we do get tired and weary and need encouragement. We have to battle thoughts and stupid ideas that are nothing more than satan's seeds of doubt and discouragement. He opposes your progress because you have something worth fighting for, the message of God's love and salvation. Your feet are hurting right about now because you are ***"KICKING SATAN'S ASS!"***

I encourage you today, to keep it up! Do not stop advancing. Your contributions of time, talents, and treasures are making a difference. Who knows, it may be this race that brings an end to satan's destructive schemes once and for all. At any moment it could all be over. Victory is imminent. Thank you for what you are doing. It is making a difference. Others are coming to life in the light of God's love and truth. Peace is being dispersed and fear dispelled with every pound of your foot. He has given you the authority through the Gospel of Peace to crush satan under your feet! Use it!

### *The Finish Line*

The last five miles were intense. The length of a mile seemed to grow longer. However, that was impossible. The distance of a mile was still the same at the end of the race as it was at the beginning. It just seemed longer. We were extremely tired, thirsty and hot. The water stops were not as frequent. It was at this point that the seasoned runners truly picked up their pace and ran out the home stretch; and, the rest of us trotted along just trying not to pass out or faint from exhaustion.

My knees and ankles were ruined. I had blisters on the balls of both feet. But I was not going to stop until I reached that finish line. I knew if I stopped for even one moment, I would not start again. It would be over for me. My determination kept me moving. I would walk at a brisk pace then run. I found out my walking had actually become faster than my running during these final few miles.

During this last leg of the race I had received a phone call from my sister. I allowed the message to go to voicemail. I knew I needed to concentrate and stay focused. My thoughts were to return the call once I was on the bus back to the hotel. Ah, the bus! I began to set my sights on the bus. This was a technique I used when training. I had to focus past the point of stopping because I always had a tendency to stop just short of the finishing point if I focused strictly on it. So, I knew in order to get to the bus, I had to pass the finish line. The bus at this point was all I wanted to see!

What I did not know then was that my sister was calling to inform me that my father had just suffered a stroke and was at the hospital in South Carolina in the intensive care unit. He had been given an invitation to speak at a church and was in the pulpit ministering when the incident occurred. That was a very traumatic moment for my family. Part of me knew that if I had answered that call, I would have found some way to get off that running path. I would have had the rescue crew drive me back to the hotel, and I would have been on the very next available flight back to South Carolina. Forget the race; I need to get to my dad!

But God in all His infinite wisdom knew that I would be receiving that call as well. He impressed me to keep running and answer later. While I ran, He began to intervene in a situation that I did not know of. He began to mend the damaged area to my father's brain where the blood clot was located. The Great Physician performed brain surgery on my dad and inserted an arterial stent in a major artery. The doctors have pictures to prove it. They could not take credit for it, for they did not operate. They charted my dad's stent as "Miraculous"! How awesome is that? When we are busy about the Kingdom work and the assignment that God has given us, He is busy taking care of those things that concern us!

One mile from the finish line, Keith and I met up with our running coach. She had been running the course back and forth looking out for her team. I bet she ran the marathon three times herself that day checking up on all of us! What a welcome sight it was to see her tiny form come into our view. We were almost there! She ran up to us congratulating us. In her most uplifting way, she asked how we would like to approach the finish line. At this time we were walking. Keith and I both wanted to run across the line. So, we grabbed each other's hand. With Arlene, our coach, in the lead we ran towards the yellow balloon-draped goal line. My head stayed lowered most of the time during this last leg. I stayed busy counting cracks in the cement or pavement. I also wanted to see any obstacles that could easily trip me up at this point. My balance was not as stable, and I was expecting my knees to give out at any moment. Loudly, Arlene encouraged me to look up. When I did, I began to focus on the sounds around me. We could hear shouting and clapping of hands. Celebratory music played in the forefront. Then something really unique happened. The announcer over the loud speaker began to shout, "Keith and Angela Henderson from Goose Creek, South Carolina, welcome! You have made it! You have finished the San Diego Marathon!"

OMG! What elation! We could not believe it! We did it! We made it! We finished the race! Once we crossed the finish line, Keith and I just embraced each other and cried. It was a moment we will never forget. We started together and finished together. We could not have accomplished it any other way. We were partners with God in this adventure. We put into practice the Proverb that says, "A cord of three strands is not easily broken." In a time of desperation, when other marriages including ours could have been afflicted and destroyed by the stress, pressure and anxiety we chose to cling to one another and remain in God. We were not only celebrating the success of a finished race, but also, the success of a new level of intimacy in our marriage.

## *Distance Strategy:*

You are doing more than just surviving. You are thriving. Allow the determination to finish become your motivation. You are closer now than when you started. If you are hurting, allow that to bring satisfaction to your heart. You are making a difference. You are kicking satan's ass. You are making great progress. Do not quit. Do not give up. It may seem to be taking longer, but the longest part of the course is actually the shortest. You are nearing the end. The goal is just in sight. Do not allow distractions to cause you to lose focus. Some calls are not meant to be answered. Ignore those things that would want you to get off course. God will take care of them; you just finish your race. There is no greater feeling than crossing the finish line of a long run. The joy is overwhelming! Congratulations, my friend! You are almost there! Remember, it's a good time to be you!

# Chapter Twelve

## Recovery and Reflections

**You will keep in perfect peace him whose mind is steadfast, because he trusts in you.
(Isaiah 26:3, NIV)**

### *Still Running*

A year and a half later, Keith and I are still running. We have made this a lifestyle, a great improvement I must say to what we were doing prior to all these events I have mentioned in this book. We realized that we could never go back to the way things had once been. We were determined to continue moving forward.

Many lessons had been learned and now came the time for application. God in His great mercy began to open doors of opportunity to bring residual income into our home. We once again entered the work force, but this time with a new attitude. We were appreciative of the positions that were afforded us. We were not victims of another person's mission, but we saw ourselves as participants in God's ultimate plan for their lives. We were the ones on a mission.

Years ago, we were easily offended with the world, its way of thinking, and lack of tolerance for the things of God. We felt persecuted and proudly testified of that in our religious meetings as we asked the rest of "Christendom" to cover us in prayer while we braved the oppressive atmosphere in the workplace. What idiots! And to think we were living this delusion that we were doing God a favor by letting the world know how offensive they were to us Christians. Now I am honored and humbled that He would trust us with His most valuable treasures of darkness. My commitment to Him is to be a light that leads them to where He is. That path should not be very far away for where I am there He is also.

Today, we see ourselves in much better form having endured this test in our lives. We have an improved financial sense. We now have a storehouse where God can make deposits of His promised blessings. You see, in the past money would come, and it would go. We made lots of money but had very little assets to show for it. We did not give God something to work with when it came to releasing His abundance. Oh, yes, we were givers, faithful givers, even extravagant givers. But, there is more to receiving God's financial abundance than just having the capacity to give it away. We learned that we had to be wise and savvy. We had to have a financial plan. We needed several depositories. God is not just going to entrust us with large amounts of money if we have not proven that we are prepared to receive it. That preparation does not include just a mere desire to have it to meet a personal need or any other need for that matter. Preparation means studying, learning, and being financially educated, not in how to get rich quick, but in how to wisely invest so that there will be an inheritance for your children and their children.

Our family has learned to love and promote peace in our home. Others who enter enjoy the serenity they feel. This is a place where we gather at the end of our busy days and relax in each other's company. We actually like being together! The children's friends like visiting as well. They feel the peace and harmony. As a matter of fact, when they come over, a "spend the night" usually turns into a "spend the weekend"!

Our opportunity for ministry has increased having wintered this storm. We find ourselves being able to truly relate to others' pain while they are in the midst of it. With compassion and empathy, we encourage them not to give up. There is always hope and a solution. We may not like the solutions; however, their application will bring the results we desire.

## *Two Witnesses of God's Divine Completion*

As I reflect on the marathon and reminisce on its lessons, I am reminded of our running time. For many runners time is of utmost importance. Time is a record that they try to beat. The winner of the San Diego Marathon, according to time keepers, ran it in two hours and nine minutes. Though that was an extraordinary feat, it still did not beat the world's record of two hours and four minutes.

Many of the runners from our team were disappointed with their run times. I heard several say that the hills added an hour to their intended time. Although I was happy just to have finished, I could relate to what they were saying. My goal time was to run the race in five hours and thirty minutes. However, Keith and I finished in six hours and twenty-three minutes (6:23). I realize for seasoned runners this time is nothing to brag about, but for someone who was happy to just reach the finish line, I was elated!

As always God is a perfect God. He never allows mere happenstance in the lives of those who walk in their purpose. Every footstep is ordered. Even a simple marathon time has significant meaning. When I studied the numbers I was amazed at what I discovered!

## *6:23*

**Six: number of man**

**Two: testimony; witness**

**Three: God; divine completion**

When I put the meanings together this is what formed: "Keith and I (man) are witnesses to the divine completion of God!" God always finishes what He starts. Philippians 1: 6 says,

*Being confident of this, that he who began a good work in you, will carry it on to completion until the day of Christ Jesus. (NIV)*

God is truly the Author and Finisher of our faith. He always finishes what He starts.

Every test has a purpose. It is to prepare us as He releases us into His kingdom for the divine purpose of our existence. I encourage you today, to rest in that fact. What you are experiencing now is preparing you for the greater things that are to come. If you are willing to go the distance, you will walk in all the blessings that determination brings. Don't stop! Keep going! You can do it! Run! Run for your life!

## *Distance Strategy:*

Never give up. God's work in you is perfect. Encourage yourself, and continue to listen to the divine guidance of His Holy Spirit. There is a way out. He will get you there! This is not a time to ignore or reject His work in you. Hang in there, and allow the molding to take place. His intricate work will have its rewards and reflect His beautiful craftsmanship. Remember, it's a good time to be you!

# *Appendix*

The following is the initial running schedule that my avid runner friend, Lesley, designed for me. I would like to share it with you. We started with a simple goal of running three miles in thirty minutes. I would accomplish this goal in 14 weeks. In actuality I reached it in 7 weeks.

I encourage you to begin somewhere doing something. Physical activity works wonders for the body, soul and spirit. It will help clear the mind and emotions of the clutter that negative energy stores. Positive reinforcement begins to flow into your heart and clarity comes to your thoughts.

If you are a non- runner like me, this is a simple plan to begin. I wish you well in all your endeavors. I know that you can do anything you set your mind to doing. I believe in the work of God in you! Enjoy!

# Week 1

| | |
|---|---|
| **Monday** | Warm up the body: Brisk walk for 5 min. Then alternate running and walking. **Run for 1 minute walk for 2 min. 3 times)**. Then brisk walk for 5 min. to cool down. Total workout time 19 min. |
| **I actually did:** | |
| **Wednesday** | Warm up the body: Brisk walk for 5 min. Then alternate running and walking. **Run for 1 minute walk for 2 min. 3 times**. Then brisk walk for 5 min. to cool down. Total workout time 19 min. |
| **I actually did:** | |
| **Friday** | Warm up the body: Brisk walk for 5 min. Then alternate running and walking. **Run for 1 minute walk for 2 min. 3 times (for total of 9 min)**. Then brisk walk for 5 min. to cool down. Total workout time 19 min. |
| **I actually did:** | |

"If you want to become the best runner you can be…start now, don't spend the rest of your life wondering if you can do it."
~Pricilla Welch

# Week 2

| Monday | Warm up the body: Brisk walk for 5 min. Then alternate running and walking. **Run for 2 minutes walk for 1 min. 3 times.** Then brisk walk for 5 min. to cool down. Total workout time 19 min. |
|---|---|
| I actually did: | |
| Wednesday | Warm up the body: Brisk walk for 5 min. Then alternate running and walking. **Run for 1 minute walk for 2 min. 4 times.** Then brisk walk for 5 min. to cool down. Total workout time 22 min. |
| I actually did: | |
| Friday | Warm up the body: Brisk walk for 5 min. Then alternate running and walking. **Run for 2 minutes walk for 1 min. 3 times.** Then brisk walk for 5 min. to cool down. Total workout time 19 min. |
| I actually did: | |

"Success is a journey, not a destination. The doing is usually more important than the outcome."
~Arthur Ashe

# Week 3

| | |
|---|---|
| **Monday** | Warm up the body: Brisk walk for 5 min. Then alternate running and walking. **Run for 3 minutes brisk walk for 2 min. 3 times.** Then brisk walk for 5 min. to cool down. Total workout time 25 min. |
| **I actually did:** | |
| **Wednesday** | Warm up the body: Brisk walk for 5 min. Then alternate running and walking. **Run for 3 minute walk for 2 min. 4 times.** Then brisk walk for 5 min. to cool down. Total workout time 30 min. |
| **I actually did:** | |
| **Friday** | Warm up the body: Brisk walk for 5 min. Then alternate running and walking. **Run for 3 minutes walk for 2 min. 3 times.** Then brisk walk for 5 min. to cool down. Total workout time 25 min. |
| **I actually did:** | |

"Perseverance is not a long race; it is many short races, one after another."
~Walter Elliott

# Week 4

| Monday | Warm up the body: Brisk walk for 5 min. Then alternate running and walking. **Run for 4 minutes brisk walk for 90 sec. 3 times.** Then brisk walk for 5 min. to cool down. Total workout time about 25 min. |
|---|---|
| I actually did: | |
| Wednesday | Warm up the body: Brisk walk for 5 min. Then alternate running and walking. **Run for 3 minute walk for 2 min. 5 times.** Then brisk walk for 5 min. to cool down. Total workout time 30 min. |
| I actually did: | |
| Friday | Warm up the body: Brisk walk for 5 min. Then alternate running and walking. **Run for 5 minutes walk for 2 min. 3 times.** Then brisk walk for 5 min. to cool down. Total workout time about 25 min. |
| I actually did: | |

"Ask yourself, Can I give more? The answer is usually yes."
~Paul Tergat – marathon world record holder (2 hours 4 Min)

# Week 5

| | |
|---|---|
| **Monday** | Warm up the body: Brisk walk for 5 min. Then alternate running and walking. **Run for 5 minutes brisk walk for 90 sec. 3 times.** Then brisk walk for 5 min. to cool down. Total workout time about 30 min. |
| **I actually did:** | |
| **Wednesday** | Warm up the body: Brisk walk for 5 min. Then alternate running and walking. **Run for 5 minute walk for 1 min. 2 times.** Then brisk walk for 5 min. to cool down. Total workout time 30 min. |
| **I actually did:** | |
| **Friday** | Warm up the body: Brisk walk for 5 min. Then alternate running and walking. **Run for 5 minutes walk for 90 sec. 3 times.** Then brisk walk for 5 min. to cool down. Total workout time about 30 min. |
| **I actually did:** | |

"Workouts are like brushing my teeth; I don't think about them, I just do them. The decision has already been made."
~Pattie Sue Plumer – U.S. Olympian

# Week 6

| Monday | Warm up the body: Brisk walk for 5 min. Then alternate running and walking. **Run for 7 minutes brisk walk for 3 min. 2 times.** Then brisk walk for 5 min. to cool down. Total workout time about 30 min. |
|---|---|
| I actually did: | |
| Wednesday | Warm up the body: Brisk walk for 5 min. Then alternate running and walking. **Run for 7 minutes walk for 90 sec. 3 times.** Then brisk walk for 5 min. to cool down. Total workout time about 30 min. |
| I actually did: | |
| Friday | Warm up the body: Brisk walk for 5 min. Then alternate running and walking. **Run for 5 minutes walk for 30 sec. 2 times.** Then brisk walk for 5 min. to cool down. Total workout time about 30 min. |
| I actually did: | |

"Hard things take time to do. Impossible things take a little longer."
~Percy Cerutty – Australian running coach

# Week 7

| | |
|---|---|
| **Monday** | Warm up the body: Brisk walk for 5 min. Then alternate running and walking. **Run for 7 minutes brisk walk for 2 min. 2 times.** Then brisk walk for 2 min. to cool down. Total workout time about 30 min. |
| **I actually did:** | |
| **Wednesday** | Warm up the body: Brisk walk for 5 min. Then alternate running and walking. **Run for 10 without stopping. Then brisk walk for 2. Run for 3 min.** Then brisk walk for 5 min. to cool down. Total workout time about 30 min. |
| **I actually did:** | |
| **Friday** | Warm up the body: Brisk walk for 5 min. Then alternate running and walking. **Run for 5 minutes walk for 30 sec. 2 times.** Then brisk walk for 5 min. to cool down. Total workout time about 30 about min. |
| **I actually did:** | |

"Believe in yourself, know yourself, deny yourself, and be humble.
~John Treacy, on the four principles of running

# Week 8

| | |
|---|---|
| **Monday** | Warm up the body: Brisk walk for 5 min. Then alternate running and walking. **Run for 8 minutes brisk walk for 2 min. then run for 10 min.** Then brisk walk for 5 min. to cool down. Total workout time about 30 min. |
| **I actually did:** | |
| **Wednesday** | Warm up the body: Brisk walk for 5 min. **Run for 15 minutes without stopping.** Then brisk walk for 10 min. to cool down. Total workout time about 30 min. |
| **I actually did:** | |
| **Friday** | Warm up the body: Brisk walk for 5 min. Then alternate running and walking. **Run for 8 minutes brisk walk for 2 min. then run for 6 min.** Then brisk walk for 5 min. to cool down. Total workout time about 30 min. |
| **I actually did:** | |

"The thing always happens that you really believe in; and the belief in a thing makes it happen."
~Frank Wright

# Week 9

| | |
|---|---|
| **Monday** | Warm up the body: Brisk walk for 5 min. Then alternate running and walking. **Run for 15 minutes brisk walk for 2 min. then run for 5 min.** Then brisk walk for 5 min. to cool down. Total workout time about 30 min. |
| **I actually did:** | |
| **Wednesday** | Warm up the body: Brisk walk for 5 min. **Run for 17 minutes without stopping.** Then brisk walk for 5 min. to cool down. Total workout time about 30 min. |
| **I actually did:** | |
| **Friday** | Warm up the body: Brisk walk for 5 min. Then alternate running and walking. **Run for 12 minutes brisk walk for 2 min. then run for 5 min.** Then brisk walk for 5 min. to cool down. Total workout time about 30 min. |
| **I actually did:** | |

"One of the greatest of all principles is that men can do what they think they can do."

~Norman Vincent Peale

Appendix

# Week 10

| Monday | Warm up the body: Brisk walk for 5 min. Then alternate running and walking. **Run for 15 minutes brisk walk for 2 min. then run for 5 min.** Then brisk walk for 5 min. to cool down. Total workout time about 30 min. |
|---|---|
| I actually did: | |
| Wednesday | Warm up the body: Brisk walk for 5 min. **Run for 20 minutes without stopping.** Then brisk walk for 5 min. to cool down. Total workout time about 30 min. |
| I actually did: | |
| Friday | Warm up the body: Brisk walk for 5 min. Then alternate running and walking. **Run for 10 minutes brisk walk for 1 min. 2 times.** Then brisk walk for 5 min. to cool down. Total workout time about 30 min. |
| I actually did: | |

"When you come to the end of your rope, tie a knot and hang on."
~Franklin Roosevelt

# Week 11

| | |
|---|---|
| **Monday** | Warm up the body: Brisk walk for 5 min. Then alternate running and walking. **Run for 20 minutes brisk walk for 1 min. then run for 5 min.** Then brisk walk for 5 min. to cool down. Total workout time about 35 min. |
| **I actually did:** | |
| **Wednesday** | Warm up the body: Brisk walk for 5 min. **Run for 23 minutes without stopping.** Then brisk walk for 5 min. to cool down. Total workout time about 30 min. |
| **I actually did:** | |
| **Friday** | Warm up the body: Brisk walk for 5 min. Then alternate running and walking. **Run for 12 minutes brisk walk for 2 min. 2 times.** Then brisk walk for 5 min. to cool down. Total workout time about 35 min. |
| **I actually did:** | |

"I've always believed that if you put in the work, the results will come. I don't do things half-heartedly because I know if I do, then I can expect half-hearted results."

~Michael Jordan

# Week 12

| Monday | Warm up the body: Brisk walk for 5 min. Then alternate running and walking. **Run for 20 minutes brisk walk for 1 min. then run for 5 min.** Then brisk walk for 5 min. to cool down. Total workout time about 35 min. |
|---|---|
| I actually did: | |
| Wednesday | Warm up the body: Brisk walk for 5 min. **Run for 25 minutes without stopping.** Then brisk walk for 5 min. to cool down. Total workout time about 35 min. |
| I actually did: | |
| Friday | Warm up the body: Brisk walk for 5 min. Then alternate running and walking. **Run for 12 minutes brisk walk for 2 min 2 times.** Then brisk walk for 5 min. to cool down. Total workout time about 35 min. |
| I actually did: | |

"To give anything less than your best is to sacrifice the gift."
~Steve Roland Prefontaine

# Week 13

| | |
|---|---|
| **Monday** | Warm up the body: Brisk walk for 5 min. Then alternate running and walking. **Run for 20 minutes brisk walk for 3 min. then run for 10 min.** Then brisk walk for 5 min. to cool down. Total workout time about 40 min. |
| **I actually did:** | |
| **Wednesday** | Warm up the body: Brisk walk for 5 min. **Run for 30 minutes without stopping.** Then brisk walk for 5 min. to cool down. Total workout time about 40 min. |
| **I actually did:** | |
| **Friday** | Warm up the body: Brisk walk for 5 min. Then alternate running and walking. **Run for 20 minutes brisk walk for 3 min. then run for 10 min.** Then brisk walk for 5 min. to cool down. Total workout time about 40 min. |
| **I actually did:** | |

"Do or do not, there is no try."
~Yoda

# Week 14

| Monday | Warm up the body: Brisk walk for 5 min. Then alternate running and walking. **Run for 30 minutes without stopping.** Then brisk walk for 5 min. to cool down. Total workout time about 40 min. |
|---|---|
| I actually did: | |
| Wednesday | Warm up the body: Brisk walk for 5 min. **Run for 15 minutes brisk walk for 2 min. 2 times.** Then brisk walk for 5 min. to cool down. Total workout time about 40 min. |
| I actually did: | |
| Friday | Warm up the body: Brisk walk for 5 min. Then alternate running and walking. **Run for 12 minutes brisk walk for 2 min. 2 times.** Then brisk walk for 5 min. to cool down. Total workout time about 35 min. |
| I actually did: | |

"My favorite part of running is the ability to be able do so."
~Lesley Green

www.ingramcontent.com/pod-product-compliance
Lightning Source LLC
LaVergne TN
LVHW041623070426
835507LV00008B/412